PARADISE

MARK CAHILL

Author of the bestsellers,
One Thing You Can't Do In Heaven,
One Heartbeat Away,
and
The Watchmen

Paradise
A Novel By Mark Cahill

April 2013

ISBN 978-0-9891065-0-4

All Scripture verses cited are from the King James Version.

Editors:
    Shari Abbott
    Sally Wilkinson

Cover Design:
    Josh Ogden, InMotion Designs
    www.inmotiondesigns.net.

Page Layout, Interior Illustrations & Final Editing:
    Brenda Nickel

Order additional copies at any bookstore
    or at www.markcahill.org.

Also available in ebook format.

Printed in the United States of America

Presented to:

14.

Finally, I am going to Paradise!! A tropical paradise! I have been waiting for this trip for a long, long time. Paradise is a place where I have been dreaming about going my entire life. No other place on earth seems to live up to the moniker, *Paradise.* But my friends have raved about this place, I have read about this place, and I just get the feeling I won't be disappointed! It is finally going to come true!

It all makes me think back to when I was a kid. I remember how my parents loved Elvis Presley! They would walk around the house and sing his songs. One of the songs that just stuck in my head when I was young has been playing like a broken record in my mind as I have been planning this trip! It was his song titled, "Paradise, Hawaiian Style." I guess that word *Paradise* has been with me from a young age!

But there was one section of the song that I have always remembered. When my parents sang it, the words just stuck with me. It went something like this: "Gee, it's great to be in that fiftieth state/the land of enchanted dreams/What an isle/where it is heaven tropical style/where love weaves a spell, it seems."

The land of enchanted dreams is what I am looking for. It might be one long flight to get to Paradise, but I know it will be worth it! I am going to make this a trip to remember. It will be a vacation like none other!

I will be the last of the four to arrive. Four college friends all meeting up for our annual golf outing. Well, it is not so much annual anymore! This will be the first time in five years we have gotten together. Amazing how work and family can cut in on annual get-togethers. Carving out some time to get away was the right decision. I need a little change of pace at this time in my life.

Let's just say I am not looking forward to this flight from Chicago to Honolulu, but if it takes 9 hours to get to Paradise, then it is worth it!

I was the only one sitting in my row and was looking forward to having it to myself, but just before the door closed, a couple walked on the plane and sat next to me. I thought, they look friendly enough. I should probably break the ice and say hello.

As they were getting settled in their seats, I said, "Hi, let me introduce myself. My name is Josh. And who might you two be?"

"We're Remo and Kaiya. Pleased to meet you, Josh."

They were wonderfully nice people and extremely friendly. This conversation will make the flight go by much faster. Now, I am fascinated by interesting names, so I thought, this will be perfect! We started chatting and the time just flew by. When I asked them why they were going to Hawaii, they said they wanted to see the place that people call *Paradise*. I knew at that moment we were going to get along just fine!

When I asked them about their family, they just stared at each other for a second. I caught the glance. They hesitated, but Remo began to speak for himself and his wife. "We had one child by birth, but he was killed in a drunk driving accident. He wasn't the one drinking. The guy in the other car was drunk, crossed the center line, and hit our son's car. There was no hope. Our son was dead at the scene. We went to all of the court hearings, the trial, and the sentencing. But something struck us as very wrong. Yes, the guy was convicted of his crime but something wasn't right. So we began to look into this young man's life. He came from a broken home, no parents that he knew of. He was a ward of the state and had a pretty extensive criminal history. He was so young, too. Only twenty years old. The same age as our son. So together, we made a decision that we were going to visit him in prison. Let's just say it was not an easy decision. I believe it was a necessary decision, but not an easy one. As we started talking to Chance, we really began to like him. He needed hope, and he didn't have any. No one else came to visit him, so we decided to continue going to see him. And believe it or not, as the visits continued, we fell in love with him. Now don't get me wrong, we so very much missed our son that died. There is no replacing him. But this young man just began to grow on us. We agreed that Chance needed a second chance. So, we decided to adopt him. He was stunned. He had no family that he knew of, tons of rejection all his life, and now the parents of the young man that he killed wanted to adopt him?! It was very overwhelming for him and very emotional. He took some time to think about it, and he decided to say, 'Yes.' Chance is now our son, and we are so happy. He gets out of prison very soon and will be coming to live with us."

"You two are serious about this, aren't you?" I replied.

"I can't even tell you how serious we are. This has literally been transforming for everyone involved. Some people have actually hated us for doing this. They think we should hold a grudge, but we just can't do that. A guy told us one day that the name *Remo* meant 'the strong one' and *Kaiya* means 'forgiveness.' He said that we needed to live those names out. So we needed to forgive Chance, and I needed to be the strong one and the leader of our home in leading by example. It has all worked out so well!"

I responded, "You two have taught me an amazing lesson about life. Everyone needs forgiveness like this. I will never forget this encounter!"

Looking out the window as we make our approach, I just can't believe how gorgeous these islands are from the air. What a view! The mountains are so steep and the water so serene and blue. The islands must be very impressive from the ground as well! It is fun to land right about sunset. The warm colors in the sky seem to make everything more golden and beautiful. But it is the sunset tomorrow that I am really looking forward to!

Remo, Kaiya, and I said our good-byes as we exchanged information. We were all excited about keeping in touch in the days to come. I knew for a fact that these were people I needed to keep around me as I continued my journey through life.

Walking into the concourse, it is good to see all of the people and stretch my legs some. Time to head to the baggage claim. I knew the other guys would be waiting on me.

"Hey, fellas!" I called out.

It sure is nice to see them once again! Michael, Daniel, and Alex had not been waiting too long. I was thankful for that!

It sure is taking a long time for these bags to show up, I thought, as I looked around and saw some commotion over by one of the baggage carousels. What is that group over there doing? It looks like they are all getting a lei put around their neck. Well, you only live once so it is time for me to mosey on over there and get me one!

"*Aloha*. Here you go, sir." They greeted me as they placed the lei over my head.

"*Mahalo*." Sure am glad I read that book on some Hawaiian phrases on the flight over! I always like to say, "thank you," so I might as well do it in their language!

"Wow! Why do Hawaiians give out leis?" I asked.

"It is a symbol of affection that we are welcoming you here to the Hawaiian Islands. We want to get your visit to Paradise started off right!"

I knew this was going to be a great trip!

"What is this one made of?"

"The name of this lei is the Maui Maunaloa Orchid Lei."

CHAPTER 14

"How would you describe its color? It is beautiful."

"It is raspberry-purple and white. And the orchid represents love, beauty, and innocence."

I just knew this was the start of something special. I think this lei is going to represent the beginning of a new chapter in my life. It will be a new beginning that is going to have a great ending!

Little does Josh know, but from the moment that he was officially welcomed to Paradise by the lei being placed around his neck, he has exactly twenty-four hours to live.

13.

"**I** *know you guys* already have the rental car, so I have already picked out the restaurant for dinner on the way back to the hotel. The world-famous Duke's in Waikiki it is!"

We are staying at the very historic Royal Hawaiian Hotel, which is just a short walk to the Outrigger Waikiki Hotel where Duke's is located. Thankfully, when we arrived at Duke's it was pretty late, so there was not a wait to be seated. What a great way to start our week in Paradise!

When our waitress, Avalon, came over, we all noticed her Notre Dame pin. "Why are you wearing that Notre Dame pin?" I asked. She said that her parents were huge Notre Dame fans when she was a kid, and that she has always loved their football team.

I responded, "That is interesting because all four of us are graduates from the University of Notre Dame!"

Avalon replied, "Does that mean I will get a big tip?"

You gotta love young people, don't you?!

"That won't be a problem with this group," I assured her. She took our drink orders and was off.

About thirty years ago, the four of us met up in college. We all lived on the same floor of Alumni Hall. The unique architecture of that dorm always enthralled us. It had gargoyles and stone carvings, and one of those stone carvings was of Knute Rockne! It was also the first dorm on campus to have an electric elevator, and we made good use of that!

Alexander (we just call him Alex) was from Texas. He was

Army ROTC and always had the desire to be in the United States Army.

Daniel was a NYC kid, and he talked like it! He was a brilliant student who wanted to go back and work on Wall Street when his schooling was done.

Michael was probably the most different of the whole bunch. He came from a very poor background, but he sure was one hard-working dude! He was at Notre Dame for pre-med and had plans to be a doctor.

And me, Josh, I got to Notre Dame because I could shoot a little hoop! I always wanted to play basketball for the Fighting Irish, and my dreams came true! Those guys would come and watch me play at the Athletic and Convocation Center. They would cheer me on when I got to play and laugh at me back at the dorm when I sat the bench. We were the best of friends, even though I wanted to punch them on a few occasions!

I was a so-so basketball player. Too many knee injuries to count. My dreams had begun to pass me by. As a kid, what I thought my life would be like was not coming to fruition. But one thing we know in life is to always have a backup plan. The good news is that my parents taught us from a young age the importance of doing well in school. So I took that training right with me to college. I knew that a good GPA would set me up for a good life. It would open many doors for me as well as give me that sheepskin from ND. So if plan number one didn't work out, I was ready with plan number two!

As we chowed down on Fresh Island Poke, Mango BBQ Baby Back Ribs, Mac Nut Chicken Katsu, and some of that famous Kimo's Original Hula Pie, we were having a great start to our vacation. It was great to reminisce and catch up since it had been a while. Face-to-face conversation is so much better than texting and emailing!

Avalon walked up and asked, "So, are you guys ready to

give me that big tip now?" Avalon definitely has a sense of humor or needs to pay some bills!

"By the way, what does *Avalon* mean?"

"It's Celtic and means 'an island paradise.'"

Why does that not surprise me! Everything is telling me that this is going to be the trip of a lifetime!

Twenty-two hours from now, Josh's trip of a lifetime will come to a screeching halt, and Paradise is going to be over for Josh.

12.

The other guys headed back to the hotel, but I've decided to walk down the famous Kalakaua Avenue for a bit. I guess the jet lag hasn't hit me yet, or I am just excited to finally be here!

This street is amazing! So many people walking and milling around on it. You can overhear so many accents. From my years in Chicago, I have heard many of these accents before: Russian, Chinese, Japanese, French, Dutch, etc. There is such a mix of people on this street. I love to meet people from other countries and learn about their culture. People are just so interesting to me, and if this is Paradise, then it should have a really good mix of people!

There are shops everywhere: Tiffany and Company, Hugo Boss, Swarovski, Coach, Chanel, and Gucci, all the way to the renowned International Market Place! You can get jewelry, Hawaiian fashions, luggage, etc., all in this one little area. People are always trying to get your attention and sell you something in the Market Place!

Boy, are my wife and kids going to be excited when they get these gifts from me! And I sure hope my wife isn't expecting a gift from Tiffany's! I better not text her a picture of that place.

I wonder why have I always enjoyed the finer things in life? I have always wanted to live in the right neighborhoods of Chicago, belong to the right country club, eat at the right restaurants, drive the right cars, have my kids in the right schools, etc.

Why have I always wanted that? I would even pay for some

of those things when they were beyond our budget. Was I just trying to keep up with the Joneses or was there something else going on?

He that hasteth to be rich hath an evil eye, and considereth not that poverty shall come upon him.   **Proverbs 28:22**

No man can serve two masters: for either he will hate the one, and love the other; or else he will hold to the one, and despise the other. Ye cannot serve God and mammon.   **Matthew 6:24**

She sure has been great to me, though. I can't think of having a better wife. I need to give her a call. It is too late back in Chicago now, so I will do that tomorrow.

Walking back to the hotel, I just know it is time for me to put my feet in that water! Take off my shoes and bury my feet in the sand. This sand is so nice. And it is like I am the only one out here on this beach taking it all in. The din of the street traffic suddenly feels like it is miles away. The warm breeze is just exhilarating. The coconut palm trees are absolutely stunning as they sway in the trade winds. The palm fronds are clacking high above me. The ocean waves are rushing to shore with their own rhythm. The moon is casting its light across the ocean. This place is just dazzling, magnificent, and exotic all at the same time! Why do I live in Chicago?! This really is Paradise!

As I am finally heading back, I see these guys on the street corner. They are passing out literature and holding up signs. I remember guys like that. I saw some of them when the four of us went down to the Sugar Bowl to watch Notre Dame vs. Georgia. I think they called them street preachers or something like that. I sure hope these guys aren't going to ruin Paradise for me.

In twenty-one hours, Josh's version of an earthly paradise will be coming to an abrupt end.

11.

Wow! What a dream! I normally don't wake up in sweats like this, but wow! I don't know if I have ever had a dream that was so vivid and so powerful. It was all so real. I don't know if I will ever forget it.

> *And it shall come to pass in the last days, saith God, I will pour out of my Spirit upon all flesh: and your sons and your daughters shall prophesy, and your young men shall see visions, and your old men shall dream dreams:* **Acts 2:17**

Was I off in another world? It was like I was behind the stage, behind the curtains, off in the wings of a very large theatre-type place. I was watching from behind. There was a huge throne with this larger than reality man/being sitting on it. This Being was incredible, and everyone's attention was riveted on Him.

> *Before the mountains were brought forth, or ever thou hadst formed the earth and the world, even from everlasting to everlasting, thou art God.* **Psalm 90:2**

He seemed so old and yet so new, all at the same time, like He was full of wisdom and truth.

> *Hast thou not known? hast thou not heard, that the everlasting God, the LORD, the Creator of the ends of the earth, fainteth not, neither is weary? there is no searching of his understanding.* **Isaiah 40:28**

He was a pure kind of clear but brilliant white. Just absolutely full of blazing light. *Holy* would be the word I would use. I have never seen anything even remotely close to that purity on planet earth. You could bleach your sheets a million times and it would never ever be like that.

And the four beasts had each of them six wings about him; and they were full of eyes within: and they rest not day and night, saying, Holy, holy, holy, Lord God Almighty, which was, and is, and is to come. **Revelation 4:8**

And his raiment became shining, exceeding white as snow; so as no fuller on earth can white them. **Mark 9:3**

There was fire, but it wasn't the kind of fire that one would normally think of. His throne was full of it. It was a purifying kind of fire. Something that tested things and made them clean by burning up the impurities around it, if that makes sense.

But then, walking down the aisle towards Him was this line. It was this long line of people. They were real people! People who had lived on the earth: every nation, tribe, language, and tongue, that kept walking up to the throne. There were these books. I couldn't tell what they were. But the people would stand there like they were being judged. Then they would depart to the left or to the right.

I beheld till the thrones were cast down, and the Ancient of days did sit, whose garment was white as snow, and the hair of his head like the pure wool: his throne was like the fiery flame, and his wheels as burning fire. A fiery stream issued and came forth from before him: thousand thousands ministered unto him, and ten thousand times ten thousand stood before him: the judgment was set, and the books were opened. I beheld then because of the voice of the great words which the horn spake: I beheld even till the beast was slain, and his body destroyed, and given to the burning flame. As concerning the rest of the beasts, they had their dominion taken away: yet their lives were prolonged for a season and time. I saw in the night visions, and, behold, one like the Son of man came with the clouds of heaven, and came to the Ancient of days, and they brought him near before him. And there was given him dominion, and glory, and a kingdom, that all people, nations, and languages, should serve him: his dominion is an everlasting dominion, which shall not pass away, and his kingdom that which shall not be destroyed.   **Daniel 7:9-14**

The sun shall be no more thy light by day; neither for brightness shall the moon give light unto thee: but the LORD shall be unto thee an everlasting light, and thy God thy glory.   **Isaiah 60:19**

This then is the message which we have heard of him, and declare unto you, that God is light, and in him is no darkness at all.   **1 John 1:5**

And whosoever was not found written in the book of life was cast into the lake of fire.   **Revelation 20:15**

And there shall in no wise enter into it any thing that defileth, neither whatsoever worketh abomination, or maketh a lie: but they which are written in the Lamb's book of life.   **Revelation 21:27**

And he shall set the sheep on his right hand, but the goats on the left. Then shall the King say unto them on his right hand, Come, ye blessed of my Father, inherit the kingdom prepared for you from the foundation of the world: **Matthew 25:33,34**

I know this is eternity. I know this is some sort of Judgment Day. I know this is real. I know this will be me someday down the road. This is all too heavy for me. Why am I having this dream tonight of all nights? I am finally at this grand hotel in Paradise, and I don't want to think about this. I need to fall back asleep if I can and get ready for the big day!

Josh doesn't realize that in twenty hours he will be walking into eternity, and Judgment Day awaits him.

10.

While those guys sleep in, I have decided to do something special today. Why? Because it is my 50th birthday! The big 5-0! Or as I am now going to call it: Hawaii Five-O!! I am so excited about this birthday. So many people told me it was a drag to hit this number. I am just not going to buy that. I have had fifty wonderful years down here, and I am planning on many more! The best is ahead of me. And I am sure not going to spend my 50th birthday in bed, no matter how much jet lag I have! So off to the world-famous Diamond Head!

Diamond Head is probably the world's most recognized volcanic crater. It's one of the iconic landmarks you can see on the island of Oahu. Some even refer to it as the Stairway to Heaven!

The literature I was reading said that the name *Diamond Head* came from British sailors when, in the 1800s, they were looking at the soil and thought they saw diamonds. What they really saw were calcite crystals that happened to look like diamonds embedded in the lava rock. That sure was a long hike for them to find out those weren't diamonds! I guess this place probably wasn't Paradise to them when they found that out!

I have arrived here pretty early this morning to beat the rush. I don't see many people around, so it should be an enjoyable hike. I am in pretty good shape for a 50 year old. Well, at least in my mind! One of my goals was to be able to dunk a basketball at forty. That didn't work out so well! So hiking Diamond Head is a good goal at 50 and something I can hopefully check off my bucket list!

This hike hasn't been bad, even though I am huffing and puffing a bit. This last section of steps looks pretty steep. I just need to go for it and remember that the view from the top is going to be worth it!

I had no clue that at the top of this mountain there was an old World War II bunker. Fascinating! I just love history. It is such a shame that we keep repeating it over and over again.

I made it! This view is breathtaking! I am stunned by how much I can see from up here. Waikiki beach is gorgeous! I can see the Royal Hawaiian Hotel where we are staying. I sure wish I could see Pearl Harbor. It was exciting and humbling to see that from the air as we were landing yesterday. Every time I gaze at the ocean, I am amazed at how clean it is and how many shades of blue there are. I can see the reefs and endless lines of waves washing ashore. Behind me, the greenery of the mountains and hills are just so lush to the eye. The air is so fresh, and the sunlight is unusually brilliant. You can just sit here and see so much. It is so refreshing to the soul to be up here! It reminds me of when I was a kid and I would sit on top of Stone Mountain. You could just lay there and look up at the sky. You could see the planes land at the Atlanta airport. You could see all of the stars and constellations, and you felt so close to them. One time the aurora borealis, or the Northern Lights, had swung so far down that there was this reddish glob of something that was so near to me, and I felt like I could grab it with my hands. I would just lay there and begin to wonder about this creation that I was in the middle of.

In the beginning God created the heaven and the earth. **Genesis 1:1**

I have always been a little adventurous. Sometimes I try to push the boundaries just a bit. It tended to get me in trouble most of my life, but it just seems to be a part of me.

So, I think I am going to step over this railing. It looks strong enough to hold on to, and the ground looks solid enough. Stepping over the line always adds a little excitement to my life. I guess living on the edge is more fun to me.

Let me take a couple of steps here. Wait a minute! This is slippery. These rocks are loose. This is not good. No! Then a hand grabbed my shoulder to steady me. I turned around. I had no clue anyone was behind me.

"Thank you so much for grabbing me."

"No worries," he said. "Probably best for you to get back on the trail."

"Good idea," I responded. When I got back on the trail, he was gone, seemingly as quickly as he had appeared. Today is probably not a good day to take chances anyways. What if I would have been seriously injured or died? Where would I have gone?

The walk down the mountain is much quicker than the walk up! Probably life will be like that, too. My next 50 years will probably go by much quicker than my first 50!

I decided to drive the long way back to the hotel, and I am captivated by the beauty of this place! Everywhere I look it is just magnificent to the eye. There is so much green here! The mansions on Kahala Avenue are just stunning. This is like Beverly Hills 90210! I would sure like to live here with my family one day. I know I can't afford it, but it sure is nice to dream.

Thou shalt not covet thy neighbour's house, thou shalt not covet thy neighbour's wife, nor his manservant, nor his maidservant, nor his ox, nor his ass, nor any thing that is thy neighbour's. **Exodus 20:17**

It is good to be back at the hotel. A quick shower, change of clothes, and off to celebrate the rest of my 50th birthday!

In thirteen hours, Josh's fiftieth birthday will be well over as he steps into eternity.

9.

"Just so you guys know, I didn't want today to be an idle use of our time, so I went ahead and made some plans for us! You have always known that I like to be organized and plan ahead, so today we have a few things on the agenda, and then tomorrow, we start golfing! And by the way, tomorrow, I have us playing golf at—are you ready, fellas?—the Waialae Country Club! Yes, that is where they hold the Sony Open. No need to thank me now. You can do that later, and I will appreciate it!!

"But for now, we're heading to the legendary North Shore! This is the place to be if you want to see some of the best waves on planet earth. And our timing couldn't be any better. Today is the last day of the Vans Triple Crown of Surfing! So not only will we be able to see some of the best waves, we will get to see some of the best surfers in the world who can ride those waves!

"Michael, you are from Miami, aren't you?"

"Yes, but what does that have to do with surfing?"

"I've seen the pictures. There's some great surfing in Florida!"

"You must have forgotten something, Josh. If you remember correctly, I told you I was poor growing up. You saw me so many times not going out to eat with the gang in college. I didn't have the funds. I was just scraping by. My parents didn't have much, and I didn't make much from the work I did. Surfboards are a little on the expensive side. It was fun to sit on the beach and watch them, but that was about as far as surfing went in my life. But I'll be honest, I'm very excited to see this surfing competition today!"

"Was it tough growing up so poor?"

"I didn't know any different, so it was just status quo for me. I will tell you though, we had a very loving family. We didn't get all caught up in the material things of the world. We knew we couldn't afford any of it, so it didn't have much of our attention. What did have our attention was each other. We had such a close knit family. That is what meant the most to us. My parents have already passed, but all of the brothers and sisters are still real close. But now that I have much more wealth being a doctor, I worry for my kids. I wonder if they will have the same life as I did, being so close to each other. They have so many gadgets now that seem to be stealing all of their time. I do think family is much more important than the things we acquire. I sure hope my kids don't miss that point growing up."

And the cares of this world, and the deceitfulness of riches, and the lusts of other things entering in, choke the word, and it becometh unfruitful. **Mark 4:19**

"Hey, fellas, look out the window," I pointed. "I know you guys recognize that as Aloha Stadium, the home of the Pro Bowl, but look above it. Yes, that is not a rainbow, but a double rainbow! That is very rare. I have never seen one before. Feast your eyes, fellas, you might not see another one of those again all the days of your life!"

And he that sat was to look upon like a jasper and a sardine stone: and there was a rainbow round about the throne, in sight like unto an emerald. **Revelation 4:3**

The drive to the North Shore was pretty quick. We saw some rather large mountains on the drive. I'm still stunned at how much green there is here! The tall jungle canopy and the vegetation filling the valleys between the steep ridges have so many shades of green. I've never seen anything like this before. It's just so exotic and captivating. The mountains that I've seen are always covered in snow, or seem kind of barren above the tree line when there is no snow. This is beautiful and refreshing, all at the same time.

As we pass the pineapple plantation along the Kamehameha Highway and approach the coffee fields, we crest the ridge to take in our first panoramic view of the North Shore. Looking into the distance, the horizon line between sky and ocean seems almost indistinguishable. We can even see the mist from the waves kicking up in the air.

"We're just about there, fellas. The North Shore!! Looks like we're not the only ones here for the Vans Surfing competition!"

As we drop into Haleiwa, the traffic begins to back up along the seven-mile miracle of world-famous surf. Good thing this road has great ocean views. It will be so good to finally find a parking spot, and then we can get out of the car and stretch our legs.

We have now arrived at the famous Banzai Pipeline! Even as a kid when I watched ABC's *Wide World of Sports*, I knew about the Pipeline, as most people called it. It was the place where the best-of-the-best went surfing. If they could surf Pipeline, they could surf anywhere!

"Look at those waves, fellas! These waves are 'going off'! That means, they're big. Look how the wind is feathering the spray off the tops of those curls! These must be twenty to thirty foot swells!"

I can feel the pounding of the surf even here! I know the surfers love those big waves, and I kind of enjoy them from either the beach or on high definition TV! I am sure glad I chose to play basketball when I was a kid, and not surfing! I think I might have wiped out way too many times!

For he commandeth, and raiseth the stormy wind, which lifteth up the waves thereof. **Psalm 107:25**

I can't even begin to explain how stunning and dazzling the scenery is! I mean it is "off the charts." It's all so different that it just heightens the senses. Everything is lit up so brightly. The sand is just so warm and soft as I walk on it. The water is so clear with brilliant shades of blue. I scan the beach and see the tops of the palm trees swaying in the distance. The land is green and beautiful to the eyes, and the sun is so warm and invigorating with a gentle breeze to boot.

He hath made every thing beautiful in his time: also he hath set the world in their heart, so that no man can find out the work that God maketh from the beginning to the end. **Ecclesiastes 3:11**

As we are walking around, I see the board with the list of former champions. I see the name "Andy Irons," and for some reason, that name rings a bell. So I asked an older gentleman standing there if he could tell me about Andy.

"Oh, now Andy was one of the all-time greats! He and Kelly Slater had a great rivalry. He grew up on Kauai, the island north of here. He was a phenomenal surfer from a young age. He had that natural instinct, but like all the champion surfers, he put tons and tons of practice into his profession. So he was good, but he also had a good work ethic."

"So is he like a legend around here?"

"People will always love Andy. It was such a shame how he died."

"He's dead?"

"Yes, he died in a hotel room in Dallas. It was a mixture of drugs. He was all of thirty-two years old. It was a real shock to so many of us who loved him. He represented Hawaii and surfing so well. It is just amazing how quickly someone can walk off this earth. They had a memorial service for him at Hanalei Bay on Kauai where they scattered his ashes over the water. Thousands of people showed up to pay their respects."

"Wow, that is so young to die."

"You better appreciate every day you have down here, sir. I am an old man, but life goes by very, very fast."

So teach us to number our days, that we may apply our hearts unto wisdom. **Psalm 90:12**

28

As we continued our walk through the crowds, we noticed there was a lot of advertising everywhere. I guess this is how they pay the bills! I noticed some advertising for Livestrong, Lance Armstrong's foundation.

"Hey, Alex, aren't you glad that you aren't Lance Armstrong right now?"

Alex responded, "I'll tell you, Josh, something never seemed right. Coming back that quickly from cancer was amazing. To come back and attain such a high level of success, by winning seven yellow jerseys in the Tour de France, was off the charts exceptional. But there were always the lingering questions. Did he dope? Did he cheat? What a fall from grace. Well, I guess we have our answer now."

"It was amazing how he kept that hidden for so many years."

But if ye will not do so, behold, ye have sinned against the LORD: and be sure your sin will find you out. **Numbers 32:23**

"When I was in the military, we did some very elite training. I mean, it was very difficult. Some days were just grueling. I couldn't even imagine doing that without being in top-notch condition—and I really mean top-notch. It always struck me, how could a man go through some very serious cancer and then not only compete in one of the most demanding and strenuous sporting events known to man, but literally dominate it for so many years. Something just didn't add up."

Michael popped in, "You guys need to slow down a bit and quit being too harsh on him. He has done some amazing things with cancer research and the like. All of those good deeds will surely outweigh his bad deeds one day."

"You really think so?" I said.

"One of the things that I have not shared much with you guys is that my mom died of cancer. It was so difficult to watch. She just emaciated away. I really think the real damage done to her was from the chemo and radiation. It seemed to eat her body up. It is tough to see your mom go out like that."

"Man, I didn't know all of that. What has been the biggest impact on you because of that?"

"Being a doctor, I try to find the answer to everything! I guess that is just how it is. So, I have done a lot of research into cancer and its effects on the body. I have also looked into how there is so much good research out there now for using natural means to get rid of cancer to avoid all of the chemotherapy and radiation. It is basically building up your immune system and then letting it fight against the cancer cells that are in you. It is almost like this body was designed to fight back against infections, cancers, diseases, etc., if it is fueled correctly to get the immune system working properly."

I will praise thee; for I am fearfully and wonderfully made: marvellous are thy works; and that my soul knoweth right well.

Psalm 139:14

"My mom died of breast cancer. You've probably seen all the pink ribbons people wear or the breast cancer walks in your city. Even the NFL had pink towels, shoes, and sweatbands this year!

"There was breast cancer in my mom's family, so she wasn't totally surprised when she was diagnosed. But as I began to do some research about the disease, I was stunned by something I found. There have been years and years of research into the connection between abortion and breast cancer. I know that might be hard to fathom because even I was really taken aback when I did this research as well. A prominent doctor by the name of Dr. Brind said that after 50 years of research there is now a significant link between abortion and breast cancer. There are tons and tons of research on the internet of these studies. So I decided to do some research on abortion and found out some very interesting statistics. Let me send them to you off of my smartphone. I really love these smartphones, but I'm sure glad we didn't have them in college. I wouldn't have gotten any work done!"

ANNUAL ABORTION STATISTICS

In 2008, approximately 1.21 million abortions took place in the U.S., down from an estimated 1.29 million in 2002, 1.31 million in 2000 and 1.36 million in 1996. From 1973 through 2008, nearly 50 million legal abortions have occurred in the U.S. (AGI).

In 2009, the highest number of reported abortions occurred in New York (119,996), Florida (81,918) and Texas (77,630); the fewest occurred in Wyoming (≤20), South Dakota (769) and North Dakota (1,290) (CDC).

The 2009 abortion ratios by state ranged from a low of 57 abortions per 1,000 live births in Mississippi (Wyoming had too few abortions for reliable tabulation) to a high of 713 abortions per 1,000 live births in NYC (CDC).

The annual number of legal induced abortions in the United States doubled between 1973 and 1979, and peaked in 1990. There was a slow but steady decline through the 1990's. Overall, the number of annual abortions decreased by 6% between 2000 and 2009, with temporary spikes in 2002 and 2006 (CDC).

The U.S. abortion rate is similar to those of Australia, New Zealand, and Sweden but higher than those of other Western European countries (NAF).

In 1998, the last year for which estimates were made, more than 23% of legal induced abortions were performed in California (CDC).

In 2005, the abortion rate in the United States was higher than recent rates reported for Canada and Western European countries and lower than rates reported for China, Cuba, the majority of Eastern European countries, and certain Newly Independent States of the former Soviet Union (CDC).

Nearly half of pregnancies among American women are unintended; about 4 in 10 of these are terminated by abortion. Twenty-two percent of all U.S. pregnancies end in abortion (AGI).[1]

Do You Know? That the taking of a human life by abortion is legal in the USA at any time throughout the entire nine months of pregnancy . . . FOR ANY REASON!

Do You Know? At [24] days after conception, a baby has a heartbeat.

Do You Know? At 6 weeks following conception, the baby's brain waves can be measured. At 8 weeks after conception, the stomach, liver, and kidneys of the baby are functioning, and fingerprints have formed. At 9 weeks, the unborn child can feel pain.

Do You Know? That 700,000 abortions are performed each year in America after 9 weeks into the pregnancy.

Do You Know? The overwhelming majority of all abortions (95%) are done as a means of birth control. Only 1% are performed because of rape or incest; 1% because of fetal abnormalities; 3% due to the mother's health problems.

Do You Know? For every two babies born, another baby dies in an abortion.

That's 1.5 million babies each year;

That's 4,000 babies every day;

That's 1 baby every 20 seconds;

That's approximately 50 million babies since 1973;

And that's just here in America.[2]

At the start of a baby's life, it looks like this dot. On day one of life, the first cell divides into two, two into four, and so on. Within five to nine days, it can be determined whether the baby is a boy or girl. At eighteen days, the heart and eyes are developing, and from twenty to twenty-four days, the heart begins to beat. Precious arms and legs are budding in twenty-eight days. By the time the baby is a "mature" thirty-day-old, it has grown ten-thousand times larger than its size on day one. On day thirty-five, if the baby could count, it would have five fingers on each hand. In forty-two days, the skeleton is formed. At ten weeks, the child can squint, swallow, pucker up its brow, and frown. Believe it or not, at eleven weeks, the baby can make complex facial expressions—even smile! Within four months, the baby can turn somersaults, swim, and grasp with its hands. If a six-month-old baby was born pre-maturely, it could survive. The baby can see, hear, and taste at month seven; eyelids also open and close. At month eight, the baby starts to get cramped. Guess what happens at month nine; the beautiful baby comes into the world. The first nine months of life are truly miraculous. Human life is precious and is to be cherished from conception to natural death.[3]

". . . [T]he number of "missing" women has risen to more than 160 million, and a journalist named Mara Hvistendahl has given us a much more complete picture of what's happened. Her book is called *Unnatural Selection: Choosing Boys Over Girls, and the Consequences of a World Full of Men.* As the title suggests, Hvistendahl argues that most of the missing females weren't victims of neglect. They were selected out of existence, by ultrasound technology and second-trimester abortion.[4]

"This is one of the things that has always fascinated me as a doctor. The feminist movement has been the number one promoter of abortion in our country, yet there are dramatically more women being aborted than men! I would think the worst thing you could do with a woman is to kill her, and of course, killing her in the womb gives her no chance to live this life. Now, across the world there are so many men that are in their marrying years and there will not be a sufficient number of women for marriage. I had never realized this until I did some research.

"I'm going to highly recommend that you guys, at some point, see the documentary *Maafa 21: Black Genocide in 21st Century America*. It was one of the most eye-opening documentaries I've ever watched. It laid out the facts that, truthfully, abortion was really a way for racial cleansing and ethnic genocide. It was for the killing of the so-called lower races. Right at 12% of the US population is black, but the black population accounts for 37% of all abortions! I can't tell you how astonished I was by these figures.

"You guys have always known that I have darker skin than you. You probably figured out that I came from a racially mixed background, even though I didn't talk much about my family to you guys in school. My father was Hispanic, and my mom was black. So when I started seeing these statistics for black abortion and abortion overall, it hit very, very close to home. I have now seen 4D ultrasound footage of a baby yawning! It was absolutely fascinating. It was a baby and nothing else, no matter what people tell you!"

"This is very interesting," Daniel interrupted. "One of my daughters went to Diablo Valley College. Yes, guys, I know what Diablo means! I've heard all the jokes about the 'devil's' college. You don't have to tell me!

Daniel continued, "She said on campus one day this group called Project Truth showed up. They were those radical prolifers. But they did something very interesting. They didn't just put up the displays with pictures of those aborted babies, but they also talked with people. My daughter told me that she had an amazing conversation with one guy in the group. He held his ground as she asked him questions. He was so kind and so loving, not only for the babies, but with her and her friends as well. They took their literature and read it. She told me that the photographs, the banners, and the brochures had a huge impact on her. She told me that she really began to think about how someday, when she is pregnant, that it will not just be a fetus inside her, but a living and growing baby."

"Believe it or not," Michael said, "When I was visiting different medical schools, one of the schools put a slide in their presentation that said, 'You are the abortion providers of tomorrow.' Something deep inside me that day knew something was wrong, and now I know why.

Michael continued, "Do you guys remember at Notre Dame when the students would put out all of those white crosses to represent aborted babies? Do you remember how they literally covered that very large grassy area? So many times I stopped and stood there, just staring and thinking. I was so thankful that my mother never aborted me."

> *Before I formed thee in the belly I knew thee; and before thou camest forth out of the womb I sanctified thee, and I ordained thee a prophet unto the nations.* **Jeremiah 1:5**

"So are you telling me, Michael, that all of those crosses represented babies that did or could have yawned in the womb?"

"That is exactly what I am saying to you, Josh. That baby is a life. You were one of those and so were each one of us. It is almost like we were knit together inside of the womb and once we were ready, we popped out!"

> *By thee have I been holden up from the womb: thou art he that took me out of my mother's bowels: my praise shall be continually of thee.* **Psalm 71:6**

Lo, children are an heritage of the LORD: and the fruit of the womb is his reward. **Psalm 127:3**

For thou hast possessed my reins: thou hast covered me in my mother's womb. **Psalm 139:13**

"Well, that led me to have a heart-to-heart with my mom," Michael continued. "I needed to find out some things as I researched how we could best treat her cancer. When I began to probe and ask some questions, she began to cry. We ended up having a good time crying together. She let me know that I should have had another brother or sister, and that she did kill one baby but kept that hidden for many years. And the anguish of not having that child stuck with her for many, many years. What she didn't realize was that abortion may have been the cause of her cancer. She then looked at me and said, 'Son, I have to tell you something. A woman knows. We just know that it is a baby inside of us, and I took that baby's life. That is probably the biggest mistake and deepest regret of my entire life.'"

"Your mom had a great son in you, Michael. She couldn't have been any prouder!"

"Thanks, Josh. We had some special times together!"

"Since this is getting pretty deep, let's do what guys always do when deep conversations come around: Eat!! Some friends back on the mainland told me that if we went to the North Shore, we had to eat at Giovanni's Shrimp Truck! Now, I know you guys might be much more sophisticated than that, but they said the Shrimp Scampi is out of this world!"

So as we were walking around, we finally located the shrimp truck and ordered our Shrimp Scampi. Yes, my friends were right. This is really good! As we were chowing down at one of their picnic tables, some other guys came over and sat right next to us. They had accents, and I love accents!

"Where are y'all from?" I asked.

"We are from Australia."

"Don't you already have beaches over there?!" They started laughing.

"Are you brothers or are you twins?"

"We are actually twins and the best of friends!"

"That is good to hear. What brings you to Hawaii?"

"To be honest, we just wanted to get away. Dealing with some things at home, and decided to just get out and explore a bit to clear our minds, and Hawaii was always one of the places that we wanted to go. So here we are!"

"That sounds like as good a reason as any to me!"

"So, what do you four guys do?"

"We have a hedge fund guy from New York City, we have a government guy from Washington, we have a doctor from Miami, and I am trying to climb the corporate ladder and conquer the world in Chicago, but it feels like I keep falling down that ladder!"

"Which one is the doctor?"

"That would be me," Michael said, as he raised his hand.

"What kind of doctor are you?"

"I'm an emergency room doctor."

"Whoa. Can we ask you a question?"

"Sure."

"Have you ever seen anything supernatural happen in your emergency room that you just could not explain in a natural way?"

"Before I answer that question, I need to ask you a question: Why do you ask me *that* question?"

"Our dad just died of cancer. That is why we are here. We needed to get away and clear our heads and do some thinking. We have been wondering if there is a God and all that. But when he died, something strange happened."

"What was that?" asked Michael.

"He said his good-byes to each one of us, and then he looked over our heads. He was looking out in the distance. It was really surreal. His eyes got big like he was seeing something. He had an almost astonished look on his face. His mouth was wide open and gaping, and then he took his last breath and died. We all thought he was seeing something, but we just weren't sure."

"That almost sounds like how Steve Jobs from Apple died."

"What do you mean?" the twins wondered.

"After his death, his sister came out about a week later and said that as he was dying, he looked over their shoulders out into the distance and said, 'Oh wow. Oh wow. Oh wow.' Then he took his last breath and died."

The twins said how that thought gave them chills running up their spines because that was so eerily similar to how their dad passed away.

"How did you know that, Michael?" the twins insisted.

"Well, since the can of worms has been opened, I guess it is time for me to lay some cards on the table. I have done a lot of research into the afterlife. And I do mean a lot. We had so many experiences with supernatural encounters that we just could not explain. They began to blow my mind. Now, you have to realize something. I began this journey as an atheist. I do not believe in God. Never have. I think we live this life, die, and become worm food. Nothing more and nothing less. Eat, drink, and be merry. For today we live, and tomorrow we die. *Carpe Diem:* Seize the day! Just like Robin Williams taught his students in the movie *Dead Poets Society:* You only get one shot here, so you better live it to the full!"

And I will say to my soul, Soul, thou hast much goods laid up for many years; take thine ease, eat, drink, and be merry. **Luke 12:19**

"Okay, Doc. Time to come clean. Give us what you have found out about these supernatural encounters. We need this to personally help us out with our dad's death."

38

"All right, you asked for it. Make sure you are ready though. Here we go. One day in the emergency room, all of us—and I do mean all of us—literally felt this presence of love move into the room. Everybody could feel it. It was literally out of this world. All of a sudden, the guy on the last table in the corner wasn't doing well. He starts flatlining. We knew there wasn't much we could do for him. It was just his time. As a doctor, you just have to realize that sometimes it is the person's time to die and that is it. You have to let them go. All of a sudden, we felt that presence move over to that bed. It was like it just hovered there. Then the guy died. The presence stayed there for a bit, and then lifted up and exited the room. As we began to talk amongst ourselves, the overall conclusion was that we thought it was the hand of God that came down, got him, and took him to heaven."

"Oh, come on, Doc. Are you serious? Did you get too much laughing gas at the dentist and were not thinking straight?" one of the twins quipped.

"Well, it doesn't end there. One of my friends flatlined on a dialysis machine, and he was gone. They zapped him with the defibrillator paddles, and lo and behold, he came back to life. He was gone for five seconds. I asked him a few weeks later if he saw anything. He told me that he most definitely did. He said that his soul exited his body and that he was hovering over his body. He could see the machine where he had flatlined. All of a sudden, he took off on a journey. He said there was this beautiful, bright light that was soothing to the eyes. There was this presence of love that just surrounded and encapsulated him. He said he saw these flowers that had the most vibrant, beautiful colors he had ever seen!"

I exclaimed, "Wow!"

"Oh, that is not the kicker," Michael explained. "He had been blind for twenty years! He had not seen anything for twenty years! So when he came back telling us about all of this stuff that he saw, we knew he must have seen it. He even said, 'If that is what death is, death is okay!!' He died five days later."

"That is so neat!" said one of the Australians. "I now know what my dad was looking at, so now I don't have to fear death since that is what will happen to all of us. Thanks for sharing that, Doc."

"Not so fast," said Michael. "That was only part of my research. As I continued studying and talking with other people, I have now met over thirty people who did not have the heavenly experience but had the hell experience."

Daniel objected, "You have got to be kidding, Michael. That can't be right. You are such a logical man. That is one of the things I have always admired about you. Hell? Come on. You must be losing it."

"You are correct, Daniel. I am logical. That is what is really blowing my mind. I never, for the life of me, thought that any of this was possible, especially the hell experience. I just thought it was religion trying to use fear to control man. They couldn't prove it, so it would be a good way to get people to follow them. It is probably much easier to control them that way."

"You have piqued my interest now, Michael," Alex said. "So if you had stories of the heavenly experiences, then I am assuming you have them of the hell experiences as well. Speak on."

"You are correct, Alex. Are you sure you guys want to hear these?"

Everyone at the table nodded their head in the affirmative. As I looked around, I could see by the look on their faces that they wanted to know, but really had no clue where this was all going to go. This really seemed to be breaking a lot of preconceived notions that probably all of us had. But if this was real and true, then deep down I knew that I needed to know this, too.

"Okay. Buckle up. I had a patient one time who was dying. I was using the defibrillator paddles on him. He died. I kept the paddles going. He came back and begged, 'No, no, don't let me die.' I kept working on him. This happened about three times. Every time he told me not to let him die. He then died. But what really got me was the expression on his face. His countenance was telling me that he was seeing something, or feeling something, and it was not good at all. He was scared, and his voice and his face were telling me that it was not good."

Daniel said, "C'mon, Michael. It was the paddles. It was the electricity from the paddles that was causing all of that. Be realistic, Michael."

"No, that is not true, Daniel. Remember I do this for a living. I have used those paddles hundreds of times. I have seen people come back from being clinically dead. I have seen this type of reaction several times, and I knew, that I knew, that I knew they were seeing something that was bad. It was written all over their faces.

"But I am not done yet. I had a friend who flatlined and was paddled back. I talked to him about his experience, and he told me that he hovered above his body and could see the flatline on the machine. He traveled to the waiting room and could tell me who was in the waiting room, what they were wearing, and what they were saying. He later related this to his relatives who had been in the waiting room, and they were stunned that he knew all of that. He then took off on a journey. At the end of the journey, he literally said there was this lake of fire that was so real that he could feel this intense heat coming off it. I wish you guys could have seen his countenance as he told me the story. This was no game to him. This was very serious business, and he kept asserting and expressing to me how real that lake of fire was."

But the fearful, and unbelieving, and the abominable, and murderers, and whoremongers, and sorcerers, and idolaters, and all liars, shall have their part in the lake which burneth with fire and brimstone: which is the second death. **Revelation 21:8**

"Do you really think he saw that?" one of the Australians asked.

"If we use some reasoning, I think we can figure this out," Michael responded.

Come now, and let us reason together, saith the LORD: though your sins be as scarlet, they shall be as white as snow; though they be red like crimson, they shall be as wool. **Isaiah 1:18**

"I really do," Michael stated. "When he told the people in the waiting room what they were wearing and saying while he was clinically dead, that is something called corroborating evidence. That would corroborate that he was literally out of his body. Once you can establish that, then the rest of the story is completely plausible. Also in my research, a 'lake of fire' was one of the most common things I heard from people.

"I had a patient tell me one day that he and a friend went to a rodeo together. His friend was actually the bull rider. His wife was a very strong Christian, and she told him that he should not go that night because something was going to happen. He just laughed at her. Neither of the guys were Christians. As the rider was strapped on the bull and the gate opened, the bull took a few steps and stumbled. It landed right on the rider. The bull rolled over and crushed him. The clowns were able to get the bull off of him. My patient then told me that he rushed out there and held his friend. He was hurt badly. He said that his friend kept saying his feet were on fire and to pull him out of the fire. He kept repeating that. Then the rider said that his legs were on fire, and he screamed for my friend to pull him up out of this fire. He then died in his arms."

And death and hell were cast into the lake of fire. This is the second death. And whosoever was not found written in the book of life was cast into the lake of fire. **Revelation 20:14,15**

"A waitress told me one time that her mom had flatlined, but they were able to revive her. She told me her mom was going down, and down, and down. People tend to describe the 'going down' experience, which is similar to what most people say about hell. Her mom kept hearing these screams. They were bloodcurdling. People were in pain. They were suffering and they obviously wanted out of there. When her mom came back, she would not talk about this experience for a long, long time. It haunted her for years because she knew what she had experienced was something real and not something imagined.

"I was chatting with some EMTs one day, and they related an experience to me. They were called to the scene of a car accident. When they arrived, there was a man who had been pulled from the wreck. They began to work on him. They needed to use the defibrillator, so they got it out and started using it on him. They said the guy flatlined. But when they used the machine, he came back. He kept saying, 'Fire, fire, flames, flames.' What is interesting is, he wasn't on fire and neither was the car. He did this on two different occasions, and then he flatlined and died."

Daniel reasoned, "See, it was the machine again. That was what was causing that sensation."

"I am not done, Daniel. When he died, both of the EMTs said they could smell a burning, sulfur smell right after he passed. They both said it was supernatural, and they both said it was hell. They had never experienced that before. But here is the kicker, they were both atheists. Neither one believed in God. But this experience had a profound effect on them. They knew it was something they could not explain with the atheistic worldview that they held."

Alex replied, "You're serious aren't you, Michael?"

"I am afraid that I am. There have been way too many experiences that I cannot explain by the natural world around us. It sure seems like it is something from the beyond. But I have saved the most astounding incident for last. I met a lady one day at my hotel on one of my trips, and we were sitting in the breakfast buffet area chatting. As we were talking, she told me that she had to tell me a story. She said that her husband flatlined and died. They tried to paddle him back, but nothing worked. So they covered him with a sheet and wheeled him out to the hallway on a gurney because he was dead. Fifteen minutes later, he sat up! This is no joke. Nothing helped him. Nobody paddled him again. He just sat right up! Well, let's just say that everyone was beyond shocked! He told his wife later that when he died, he started going down this dark tunnel. I have actually heard about this dark tunnel from more than one person. It was not a white light tunnel, but a dark tunnel that went down. He said he kept going down, but the whole time he kept hearing this weeping and wailing. The screams of the people just haunted him, he said. It was some serious pain that they were in. He kept going lower and lower in this tunnel when all of a sudden, two hands of light grabbed him. He told his wife he knew instantly that it was Jesus. He didn't say how he knew that, but he just knew it. The hands started pulling him up, and up, and up. And when he hit the top of the tunnel, he sat straight up on the gurney! She told me that she asked her husband the question: 'What was the worst part of that experience?' And he responded to her that the worst part was that he couldn't bring anyone out with him. That they were stuck there for eternity."

And cast ye the unprofitable servant into outer darkness: there shall be weeping and gnashing of teeth. **Matthew 25:30**

I said, "Okay, fellas, I think we need to stop here. I am getting goose bumps on my arms, and the hair is standing up on the back of my neck."

"You are serious, Doc? No joke?" one of the Australians said.

"I am afraid so, gentlemen. So when your dad was looking over your heads and saying, 'Oh, wow,' my guess is that it could have been good, or it could have been bad."

"You have given us so much to think about, Michael. Thank you. I am so glad that we ran into you guys. By the way, do you think this is what they call a divine appointment?"

"I wouldn't go that far, fellas. Remember, I am an atheist! But the more and more I search this out, the more I am doubting my position."

I chimed in and said, "One of the traditions around here, that my friends told me about, is that we are supposed to write something on the shrimp truck and take a photo. Now, I am not much for writing on someone's vehicle, but I do want to take a group photo because I get the feeling that I never want to forget you guys!"

Josh doesn't realize it, but he is nine hours away from stepping into eternity and having a real experience he will never come back from.

8.

As we were walking past the beach one more time, I looked at those waves again, the beach, the gorgeous blue sky, and just began to wonder, where did all this come from? The surfers were amazing! They were taking some nasty spills though. I am sure someone can die surfing just like they can die in a car accident. If that happened, what would they see? Would it be that warm, soothing light, or would they hear the screams of the damned and see that Lake of Fire? Never thought I would be thinking about this on my birthday.

We were getting close to the car, when I saw a man handing out some materials across the street. I told the guys that I would be right back. As I approached the man, he asked, "Did you get one of these?" He handed me a postcard kind of thing with some writing on it.

"What is this?" I asked.

He explained, "It's a gospel tract."

"What is that?"

He told me that *gospel* means "good news" and that we all need some good news. Well, he was sure right about that after hearing all of those "hell" experiences that Michael told us!

I thanked him and began to walk away.

Then he asked, "Can I say something to you?"

"Sure."

"I just want to let you know that I thank God for you."

Wow. I had never had anyone say that to me before.

"What is your name?" I asked.

"Darrel."

"You mean that, don't you, Darrel?"

"Yes, I most definitely do."

I could tell from his demeanor, his voice, and his countenance, he most definitely did. I think I will always remember that brief encounter.

As we were driving away, I was contemplating what Darrel had said, when something caught my eye.

"Hey, Alex, pull over," I blurted. "That is Ted's Bakery. Some friends told me that if I go to the North Shore, I needed to stop in there and get some 'chocolate happy something'!"

As we pulled over and walked into Ted's, they told us it was their Chocolate Haupia Pie we were looking for and not a "chocolate happy something"! No surprise now why the locals were laughing at me! *Haupia* is the traditional coconut milk-based dessert. It is called pudding, but it is really more like gelatin. I could already tell this would be a good finish after having that Shrimp Scampi! And it is my 50th birthday, and I am going to celebrate! So we all ordered some to go.

As we got in the car and started heading back, I looked at that gospel tract, and it brought back an interesting memory.

"Hey, guys. Do you remember when we all went down to the Sugar Bowl eons ago? We were walking into the French Quarter, and there were these guys standing out front handing out pieces of literature."

"You remember the strangest things, Josh!" Alex chimed in.

"One guy stuck something right into my hand. I have always hated to litter, so that paper went in my pocket. When we arrived back at the hotel late that evening, I pulled it out of my pocket and read it. Now, I don't remember what it said all these years later, but I do remember something about it. It had something on there called the Romans Road. That is what stuck in my head. I just googled it on my phone. Let me read this to you guys."

THE ROMANS ROAD

Romans 3:23 "For all have sinned, and come short of the glory of God;"

Romans 6:23 "For the wages of sin is death; but the gift of God is eternal life through Jesus Christ our Lord."

Romans 5:8 "But God commendeth his love toward us, in that, while we were yet sinners, Christ died for us."

Romans 10:13 "For whosoever shall call upon the name of the Lord shall be saved."

Romans 10:9,10 "That if thou shalt confess with thy mouth the Lord Jesus, and shalt believe in thine heart that God hath raised him from the dead, thou shalt be saved. For with the heart man believeth unto righteousness; and with the mouth confession is made unto salvation."

Romans 5:1 "Therefore being justified by faith, we have peace with God through our Lord Jesus Christ:"

Romans 8:1 "There is therefore now no condemnation to them which are in Christ Jesus, who walk not after the flesh, but after the Spirit."

Romans 8:38,39 "For I am persuaded, that neither death, nor life, nor angels, nor principalities, nor powers, nor things present, nor things to come, Nor height, nor depth, nor any other creature, shall be able to separate us from the love of God, which is in Christ Jesus our Lord."

"Oh great. Just what a Jewish guy wants to hear: Jesus, Jesus, Jesus!" Daniel objected. "Those statements also make a huge assumption, Josh. You are assuming the Bible is true. Why would you make that assumption by reading that to us? You and I both know that it was passed down by word of mouth, it has errors in it, evolution has disproved it, and we can't trust some silly book that was written so many years ago."

Michael said, "Well, I hate to interrupt your discussion here, since I did most of the talking at lunch today, but when I went on this search, part of it had to include the Bible. It has literally sold more copies than any other book in the history of the world. I also found out it is the most shoplifted of all books as well!! It is translated in over 1200 different languages. And, since it mentions all kinds of animals, but never mentions cats—and you guys know I don't like cats—we should probably read this book! And since we doctors tend to not like lawyers so much and only two lawyers are ever mentioned in the Bible, this is probably a book we should memorize one day!! There is just something about this book that has fascinated people throughout the ages."

Alex said, "That is all fine and dandy, Michael, but that doesn't mean it is true."

"Thanks for saying that, Alex, because you are so correct. Here is the best-selling book in the history of the world, and we won't even teach it in our schools! I had to wonder why that is? You have to go to a private school to learn about it, and even then you can't be sure that what they are teaching about it is accurate, because so many teachers seem to be spending more time denigrating the book rather than finding out its truths.

Michael continued, "Okay, all of you guys make sure you have your phones turned on. Alex, you keep your eyes on the road, and you can just listen to some of this information. You guys know me—I am pretty meticulous. You do remember how you always wanted to look at my notes when we were studying for exams, don't you?! As I was doing my research, I kept files on certain subjects. So, I'm going to send some files to your phones. You can open them up as well, and we can take a look at them. I was watching some videos by this guy, Dr. Ron Carlson. I have always loved intellectual people who put in the research to defend their position. I really loved his academic background and his passion for truth.

"Just a second. Okay, you should have the file now: *Is The Bible True?* All right, let's open it."

IS THE BIBLE TRUE?

During a question and answer session at a recent speaking engagement, a university student asked me, "Why do you believe that the Bible is the inspired word of God?" Now this is a very interesting question, and probably one of the most important questions any Christian could ask themselves. What is so special, so unique about the Bible that Christians believe it is literally the inspired word of God?

In answering this student's question, I encouraged him to consider the following facts about the Bible:

First, the Bible is not just one single book. This is a more common misconception than many people realize, especially with people who do not come from a Judeo-Christian background. Rather than being a single book, the Bible is actually a collection of 66 books, which is called the canon of scriptures. These 66 books contain a variety of genres: history, poetry, prophecy, wisdom literature, letters, and apocalyptic, just to name a few.

Second, these 66 books were written by 40 different authors. These authors came from a variety of backgrounds: shepherds, fishermen, doctors, kings, prophets and others. And most of these authors never knew one another personally.

Third, these 66 books were written over a period of 1500 years. Yet again, this is another reminder that many of these authors never knew or collaborated with one another in writing these books.

Fourth, the 66 books of the Bible were written in 3 different languages. In the Bible we have books that were written in the ancient languages of Hebrew, Greek, and Aramaic; a reflection of the historical and cultural circumstances in which each of these books were written.

And finally, these 66 books were written on 3 different continents: Africa, Asia, and Europe. Once again, this is a testament to the varied historical and cultural circumstances of God's people.

Think about the above realities: 66 books, written by 40 different authors, over 1500 years, in 3 different languages, on 3 different continents. What's more, this collection of books shares a common storyline—the creation, fall, and redemption of God's people; a common theme—God's universal love for all of humanity; and a common message—salvation is available to all who repent of their sins and commit to following God with all of their heart, soul, mind, and strength. In addition to sharing these commonalities, these 66 books contain no historical errors or contradictions. God's word truly is an amazing collection of writings!

After I had shared the above facts with this student, I offered him the following challenge: I said to him, "If you do not believe that the Bible is the inspired word of God, if you do not believe that the Bible is of a supernatural origin, then I challenge you to a test." I said to the student, "I challenge you to go to any library in the world, you can choose any library you like, and find 66 books which match the characteristics of the 66 books in the Bible. You must choose 66 books, written by 40 different authors, over 1500 years, in 3 different languages, written on 3 different continents. However, they must share a common storyline, a common theme and a common message, with no historical errors or contradictions." I went on to say, "If you can produce such a collection of books, I will admit that the Bible is not the inspired word of God." The student's reply was almost instantaneous; he emphatically stated, "But that's impossible!"

"But that's impossible!" It truly is impossible, for any collection of human writings. However, the Bible passes this test. The Bible contains 66 books, written by 40 different authors, over 1500 years, in 3 different languages, on 3 different continents, with no historical errors or contradictions. The entire Bible, from Genesis to Revelation, bears the mark of Divine inspiration.[5]

"That is pretty convincing," Alex replied.

"One of the things I had always thought was that the Bible was and had been written by men," responded Michael. "Now we know that men took pen to paper or parchment and wrote it down, but the more I researched it, the more it seemed they were not the authors of the book, but that God was. And as an atheist, that totally challenged my thinking."

All scripture is given by inspiration of God, and is profitable for doctrine, for reproof, for correction, for instruction in righteousness:
2 Timothy 3:16

Knowing this first, that no prophecy of the scripture is of any private interpretation. For the prophecy came not in old time by the will of man: but holy men of God spake as they were moved by the Holy Ghost. **2 Peter 1:20,21**

"One other thing that kept hitting me was that the book kept saying, 'Thus saith the Lord.' It says that over 400 times! In no way, shape, or form was this book claiming human authorship. Matter of fact, it was claiming just the opposite! It was saying that these were the words of God Himself. Nothing short of that, meaning these are the words He wanted communicated to us. I found that nothing less than astonishing!"

"Now hold up a minute," Daniel said. "I can sit here and tell you that God told me to tell you to sign over your trust fund, IRA, and deed to your house to me, but that doesn't mean God said that! You have to have much more convincing evidence than that."

"One thing I have always liked about you, Daniel, is that you are a thinker!" Michael responded. "You are so logical. That is one reason why you are an excellent hedge fund manager! Thanks for doing such a good job with my money! Just don't turn into a Bernie Madoff on me!! But since you know me, too, you will not be surprised that I have a little bit more to share with you!"

IN WHAT WAYS HAVE THE DISCOVERIES OF ARCHAEOLOGY VERIFIED THE RELIABILITY OF THE BIBLE?

Over the years there have been many criticisms leveled against the Bible concerning its historical reliability. These criticisms are usually based on a lack of evidence from outside sources to confirm the Biblical record. Since the Bible is a religious book, many scholars take the position that it is biased and cannot be trusted unless we have corroborating evidence from extra-Biblical sources. In other words, the Bible is guilty until proven innocent, and a lack of outside evidence places the Biblical account in doubt.

This standard is far different from that applied to other ancient documents, even though many, if not most, have a religious element. They are considered to be accurate, unless there is evidence to show that they are not. Although it is not possible to verify every incident in the Bible, the discoveries of archaeology since the mid-1800s have demonstrated the reliability and plausibility of the Bible narrative.

Here are some examples:

The discovery of the Ebla archive in northern Syria in the 1970s has shown the Biblical writings concerning the Patriarchs to be viable. Documents written on clay tablets from around 2300 B.C. demonstrate that personal and place names in the Patriarchal accounts are genuine. The name "Canaan" was in use in Ebla, a name critics once said was not used at that time and was used incorrectly in the early chapters of the Bible. The word tehom ("the deep") in Genesis 1:2 was said to be a late word demonstrating the late writing of the creation story. "Tehom" was part of the vocabulary at Ebla, in use some 800 years before Moses. Ancient customs reflected in the stories of the Patriarchs have also been found in clay tablets from Nuzi and Mari.

The Hittites were once thought to be a Biblical legend, until their capital and records were discovered at Bogazkoy, Turkey.

Many thought the Biblical references to Solomon's wealth were greatly exaggerated. Recovered records from the past show that wealth in antiquity was concentrated with the king and Solomon's prosperity was entirely feasible.

It was once claimed there was no Assyrian king, named Sargon as recorded in Isaiah 20:1, because this name was not known in any other record. Then, Sargon's palace was discovered in Khorsabad, Iraq. The very event mentioned in Isaiah 20, his capture of Ashdod, was recorded on the palace walls. What is more, fragments of a stela memorializing the victory were found at Ashdod itself.

Another king who was in doubt was Belshazzar, king of Babylon, named in Daniel 5. The last king of Babylon was Nabonidus according to recorded history. Tablets were found showing that Belshazzar was Nabonidus' son who served as co-regent in Babylon. Thus, Belshazzar could offer to make Daniel "third highest ruler in the kingdom" (Daniel 5:16) for reading the handwriting on the wall, the highest available position. Here we see the "eye-witness" nature of the Biblical record, as is so often brought out by the discoveries of archaeology.[6]

"One other article I was reading said there were over 25,000 archaeological finds in the Middle East that had to do with people, places, and events, and not one of them disproved a Biblical fact. Matter of fact, they all showed the book to be true."

"That is nice," Alex stated. "But that still doesn't prove that the Bible is the inspired Word of God. If someone is going to commit their life to this book, this God, His Son, etc., they are going to need just a wee bit more information than that! We are talking about a commitment here that could affect our eternal destinations and should radically change how we live our lives here on planet earth. This should not be a flippant decision. There should be some overwhelming proof, or it is literally just a waste of our time."

Michael came back with, "Excellent point, Alex. And you are so correct. When I investigated all of this, the information seemed well and good. But that would not be enough to push me over the edge, so to speak, to become a believer. I needed more. My rational mind kept telling me there had to be more to this, and if there wasn't, then I was wasting my time. And you guys know me well enough. I am a workaholic. I try to accomplish a lot. I want things done right. So if I am heading down this path on my search, I do not want it to be a misuse of my time. But since this is about eternity, it is worth putting forth a good effort into finding some things out.

"There is a trump card that I have not told you about. There was something on my search that just threw me for a loop. It let me know that the Bible could never have been written by man, but had to be from the hand of God!"

Daniel replied, "All right, Michael. If you have that trump card, it is time to play it. There is no sense leaving that in your hand when you have already laid out all of these other cards on the table. The cards you have played are extremely interesting, but go ahead and play the card you have been wanting to play, and let's see if you can win this hand."

"This all comes down to something called *prophecy*. A prophecy is basically 'a prediction of the future.' Now any person can do that, even us. We see it all the time from Nostradamus, Edgar Cayce, Jeane Dixon and the magazines when we are checking out at the grocery store. But that is not the kicker. The key is if it becomes a fulfilled prophecy. So if you say something is going to happen and it does happen, that is huge in my book. And if you can do that over and over and over again, I can't deny the reality at that point.

"Okay, check your phones. Here comes the trump card!"

FULFILLED PROPHECY: EVIDENCE FOR THE RELIABILITY OF THE BIBLE

Unique among all books ever written, the Bible accurately foretells specific events, in detail, many years, sometimes centuries, before they occur. Approximately 2500 prophecies appear in the pages of the Bible, about 2000 of which already have been fulfilled to the letter—no errors.

(The remaining 500 or so reach into the future and may be seen unfolding as days go by.) Since the probability for any one of these prophecies having been fulfilled by chance averages less than one in ten (figured very conservatively) and since the prophecies are for the most part independent of one another, the odds for all these prophecies having been fulfilled by chance without error is less than one in 10^{2000} (that is 1 with 2000 zeros written after it)!

God is not the only one, however, who uses forecasts of future events to get people's attention. Satan does, too. Through clairvoyants (such as Jeanne Dixon and Edgar Cayce), mediums, spiritists, and others come remarkable predictions, though rarely with more than about 60 percent accuracy, never with total accuracy. Messages from Satan, furthermore, fail to match the detail of Bible prophecies, nor do they include a call to repentance.

The acid test for identifying a prophet of God is recorded by Moses in Deuteronomy 18:21-22. According to this Bible passage (and others), God's prophets, as distinct from Satan's spokesmen, are 100 percent accurate in their predictions. There is no room for error.

As economy does not permit an explanation of all the Biblical prophecies that have been fulfilled, what follows is a discussion of a few that exemplify the high degree of specificity, the range of projection, and/or the "supernature" of the predicted events. Readers are encouraged to select others, as well, and to carefully examine their historicity.

(1) Some time before 500 B.C., the prophet Daniel proclaimed that Israel's long-awaited Messiah would begin his public ministry 483 years after the issuing of a decree to restore and rebuild Jerusalem (Daniel 9:25-26). He further predicted that the Messiah would be "cut off," killed, and that this event would take place prior to a second destruction of Jerusalem. Abundant documentation shows that these prophecies were perfectly fulfilled in the life (and crucifixion) of Jesus Christ. The decree regarding the restoration of Jerusalem was issued by Persia's King Artaxerxes to the Hebrew priest Ezra in 458 B.C.; 483 years later the ministry of Jesus Christ began in Galilee. (Remember that due to calendar changes, the date for the start of Christ's ministry is set by most historians at about 26 A.D. Also note that from 1 B.C. to 1 A.D. is just one year.) Jesus' crucifixion occurred only a few years later, and about four decades later, in 70 A.D. came the destruction of Jerusalem by Titus. *(Probability of chance fulfillment = 1 in 10^5.)*

(2) In approximately 700 B.C., the prophet Micah named the tiny village of Bethlehem as the birthplace of Israel's Messiah (Micah 5:2). The fulfillment of this prophecy in the birth of Christ is one of the most widely known and widely celebrated facts in history. *(Probability of chance fulfillment = 1 in 10^5.)*

(3) In the fifth century B.C., a prophet named Zechariah declared that the Messiah would be betrayed for the price of a slave—thirty pieces of silver according to Jewish law, and also that this money would be used to buy a burial ground for Jerusalem's poor foreigners (Zechariah 11:12-13). Bible writers and secular historians both record thirty pieces of silver as the sum paid to Judas Iscariot for betraying Jesus, and they indicate that the money went to purchase a "potter's field," used—just as predicted—for the burial of poor aliens (Matthew 27:3-10). *(Probability of chance fulfillment = 1 in 10^{11}.)*

(4) Some 400 years before crucifixion was invented, both Israel's King David and the prophet Zechariah described the Messiah's death in words that perfectly depict that mode of execution. Further, they said that the body would be pierced and that none of the bones would be broken, contrary to customary procedure in cases of crucifixion (Psalm 22 and 34:20; Zechariah 12:10). Again, historians and New Testament writers confirm the fulfillment: Jesus of Nazareth died on a Roman cross, and his extraordinarily quick death eliminated the need for the usual breaking of bones. A spear was thrust into his side to verify that he was, indeed, dead. *(Probability of chance fulfillment = 1 in 10^{13}.)*

(5) The prophet Isaiah foretold that a conqueror named Cyrus would destroy seemingly impregnable Babylon and subdue Egypt along with most of the rest of the known world. This same man, said Isaiah, would decide to let the Jewish exiles in his territory go free without any payment of ransom (Isaiah 44:28; 45:1; and 45:13). Isaiah made this prophecy 150 years before Cyrus was born, 180 years before Cyrus performed any of these feats (and he did, eventually, perform them all), and 80 years before the Jews were taken into exile. *(Probability of chance fulfillment = 1 in 10^{15}.)*

(6) Mighty Babylon, 196 miles square, was enclosed not only by a moat, but also by a double wall 330 feet high, each part 90 feet thick. It was said by unanimous popular opinion to be indestructible, yet two Bible prophets declared its doom. These prophets further claimed that the ruins would be avoided by travelers, that the city would never again be inhabited, and that its stones would not even be moved for use as building material (Isaiah 13:17-22 and Jeremiah 51:26,43). Their description is, in fact, the well-documented history of the famous citadel. *(Probability of chance fulfillment = 1 in 10^9.)*

(7) The exact location and construction sequence of Jerusalem's nine suburbs was predicted by Jeremiah about 2600 years ago. He referred to the time of this building project as "the last days," that is, the time period of Israel's second rebirth as a nation in the land of Palestine (Jeremiah 31:38-40). This rebirth became history in 1948, and the construction of the nine suburbs has gone forward precisely in the locations and in the sequence predicted. *(Probability of chance fulfillment = 1 in 10^{18}.)*

(8) The prophet Moses foretold (with some additions by Jeremiah and Jesus) that the ancient Jewish nation would be conquered twice and that the people would be carried off as slaves each time, first by the Babylonians (for a period of 70 years), and then by a fourth world kingdom (which we know as Rome). The second conqueror, Moses said, would take the Jews captive to Egypt in ships, selling them or giving them away as slaves to all parts of the world. Both of these predictions were fulfilled to the letter, the first in 607 B.C. and the second in 70 A.D. God's spokesmen said, further, that the Jews (would remain scattered throughout the entire world for many generations, but without becoming assimilated by the peoples of other nations, and that the Jews would one day return to the land of Palestine to re-establish for a second time their nation (Deuteronomy 29; Isaiah 11:11-13; Jeremiah 25:11; Hosea 3:4-5; and Luke 21:23-24). This prophetic statement sweeps across 3500 years of history to its complete fulfillment—in our lifetime.
(Probability of chance fulfillment = 1 in 10^{20}.)

(9) Jeremiah predicted that despite its fertility and accessibility of its water supply, the land of Edom (today a part of Jordan) would become a barren, uninhabited wasteland (Jeremiah 49:15-20; Ezekiel 25:12-14). His description accurately tells the history of that now bleak region.
(Probability of chance fulfillment = 1 in 10^{5}.)

(10) Joshua prophesied that Jericho would be rebuilt by one man. He also said that the man's eldest son would die when the reconstruction began and that his youngest son would die when the work reached completion (Joshua 6:26). About five centuries later this prophecy found its fulfillment in the life and family of a man named Hiel (1 Kings 16:33-34).
(Probability of chance fulfillment = 1 in 10^{7}.)

(11) The day of Elijah's supernatural departure from Earth was predicted unanimously—and accurately, according to the eye-witness account—by a group of fifty prophets (2 Kings 2:3-11).

(Probability of chance fulfillment = 1 in 10^9.)

(12) Jahaziel prophesied that King Jehoshaphat and a tiny band of men would defeat an enormous, well-equipped, well-trained army without even having to fight. Just as predicted, the King and his troops stood looking on as their foes were supernaturally destroyed to the last man (2 Chronicles 20).

(Probability of chance fulfillment = 1 in 10^8.)

(13) One prophet of God (unnamed, but probably Shemiah) said that a future king of Judah, named Josiah, would take the bones of all the occultic priests (priests of the "high places") of Israel's King Jeroboam and burn them on Jeroboam's altar (1 Kings 13:2 and 2 Kings 23:15-18). This event occurred approximately 300 years after it was foretold.

(Probability of chance fulfillment = 1 in 10^{13}.)

Since these thirteen prophecies cover mostly separate and independent events, the probability of chance occurrence for all thirteen is about 1 in 10^{138} (138 equals the sum of all the exponents of 10 in the probability estimates above). For the sake of putting the figure into perspective, this probability can be compared to the statistical chance that the second law of thermodynamics will be reversed in a given situation (for example, that a gasoline engine will refrigerate itself during its combustion cycle or that heat will flow from a cold body to a hot body)—that chance = 1 in 10^{80}. Stating it simply, based on these thirteen prophecies alone, the Bible record may be said to be vastly more reliable than the second law of thermodynamics. Each reader should feel free to make his own reasonable estimates of probability for the chance fulfillment of the prophecies cited here. In any case, the probabilities deduced still will be absurdly remote.

Given that the Bible proves so reliable a document, there is every reason to expect that the remaining 500 prophecies, those slated for the "time of the end," also will be fulfilled to the last letter. Who can afford to ignore these coming events, much less miss out on the immeasurable blessings offered to anyone and everyone who submits to the control of the Bible's author, Jesus Christ? Would a reasonable person take lightly God's warning of judgment for those who reject what they know to be true about Jesus Christ and the Bible, or who reject Jesus' claim on their lives?[7]

"That is extremely powerful evidence," I said.

"Don't forget something," Michael responded. "Remember, I said that the Bible keeps saying over and over that these are the words of God. So, the book is saying that God is making these predictions, and these predictions keep coming true. And they don't just come true, but they come true with 100 percent accuracy! Every little detail. 2000 times! Nothing was predicted that hasn't come true to this point. To me, that is evidence that is off the charts!"

"In that document, it kept mentioning the Messiah. Now I remember from some college classes that they referred to Jesus as the Messiah. Are there any prophecies for Him and His life, Michael?" I asked.

"Great deduction, Josh! I knew I always liked you!

"All right, check your phones. Here it comes!"

44 Prophecies Jesus Christ Fulfilled

	Prophecies About Jesus	Old Testament Scripture	New Testament Fulfillment
1	Messiah would be born of a woman.	Genesis 3:15	Matthew 1:20 Galatians 4:4
2	Messiah would be born in Bethlehem.	Micah 5:2	Matthew 2:1 Luke 2:4-6
3	Messiah would be born of a virgin.	Isaiah 7:14	Matthew 1:22-23 Luke 1:26-31
4	Messiah would come from the line of Abraham.	Genesis 12:3 Genesis 22:18	Matthew 1:1 Romans 9:5
5	Messiah would be a descendant of Isaac.	Genesis 17:19 Genesis 21:12	Luke 3:34
6	Messiah would be a descendant of Jacob.	Numbers 24:17	Matthew 1:2
7	Messiah would come from the tribe of Judah.	Genesis 49:10	Luke 3:33 Hebrews 7:14
8	Messiah would be heir to King David's throne.	2 Samuel 7:12-13 Isaiah 9:7	Luke 1:32-33 Romans 1:3
9	Messiah's throne will be anointed and eternal.	Psalm 45:6-7 Daniel 2:44	Luke 1:33 Hebrews 1:8-12
10	Messiah would be called Immanuel.	Isaiah 7:14	Matthew 1:23
11	Messiah would spend a season in Egypt.	Hosea 11:1	Matthew 2:14-15
12	A massacre of children would happen at Messiah's birthplace.	Jeremiah 31:15	Matthew 2:16-18
13	A messenger would prepare the way for Messiah.	Isaiah 40:3-5	Luke 3:3-6
14	Messiah would be rejected by his own people.	Psalm 69:8 Isaiah 53:3	John 1:11 John 7:5
15	Messiah would be a prophet.	Deuteronomy 18:15	Acts 3:20-22
16	Messiah would be preceded by Elijah.	Malachi 4:5-6	Matthew 11:13-14
17	Messiah would be declared the Son of God.	Psalm 2:7	Matthew 3:16-17
18	Messiah would be called a Nazarene.	Isaiah 11:1	Matthew 2:23
19	Messiah would bring light to Galilee.	Isaiah 9:1-2	Matthew 4:13-16
20	Messiah would speak in parables.	Psalm 78:2-4 Isaiah 6:9-10	Matthew 13:10-15, 34-35

21	Messiah would be sent to heal the brokenhearted.	Isaiah 61:1-2	Luke 4:18-19
22	Messiah would be a priest after the order of Melchizedek.	Psalm 110:4	Hebrews 5:5-6
23	Messiah would be called King.	Psalm 2:6 Zechariah 9:9	Matthew 27:37 Mark 11:7-11
24	Messiah would be praised by little children.	Psalm 8:2	Matthew 21:16
25	Messiah would be betrayed.	Psalm 41:9 Zechariah 11:12-13	Luke 22:47-48 Matthew 26:14-16
26	Messiah's price money would be used to buy a potter's field.	Zechariah 11:12-13	Matthew 27:9-10
27	Messiah would be falsely accused.	Psalm 35:11	Mark 14:57-58
28	Messiah would be silent before his accusers.	Isaiah 53:7	Mark 15:4-5
29	Messiah would be spat upon and struck.	Isaiah 50:6	Matthew 26:67
30	Messiah would be hated without cause.	Psalm 35:19 Psalm 69:4	John 15:24-25
31	Messiah would be crucified with criminals.	Isaiah 53:12	Matthew 27:38 Mark 15:27-28
32	Messiah would be given vinegar to drink.	Psalm 69:21	Matthew 27:34 John 19:28-30
33	Messiah's hands and feet would be pierced.	Psalm 22:16 Zechariah 12:10	John 20:25-27
34	Messiah would be mocked and ridiculed.	Psalm 22:7-8	Luke 23:35
35	Soldiers would gamble for Messiah's garments.	Psalm 22:18	Luke 23:34 Matthew 27:35-36
36	Messiah's bones would not be broken.	Exodus 12:46 Psalm 34:20	John 19:33-36
37	Messiah would be forsaken by God.	Psalm 22:1	Matthew 27:46
38	Messiah would pray for his enemies.	Psalm 109:4	Luke 23:34
39	Soldiers would pierce Messiah's side.	Zechariah 12:10	John 19:34
40	Messiah would be buried with the rich.	Isaiah 53:9	Matthew 27:57-60
41	Messiah would resurrect from the dead.	Psalm 16:10 Psalm 49:15	Matthew 28:2-7 Acts 2:22-32
42	Messiah would ascend to heaven.	Psalm 24:7-10	Mark 16:19 Luke 24:51
43	Messiah would be seated at God's right hand.	Psalm 68:18 Psalm 110:1	Mark 16:19 Matthew 22:44
44	Messiah would be a sacrifice for sin.	Isaiah 53:5-12	Romans 5:6-8

8

Daniel replied, "Okay, I think we need to stop this. I have been taught by my rabbis for years that Jesus is not the Messiah. I have learned it in Hebraic school as well. My wife and I are of the Reform Jewish movement. Many people say it is the more liberal side of Judaism. We do not hold to Jesus being the Messiah like these Messianic Jews, or so-called Completed Jews do. Matter of fact, I find it highly offensive to what I have been taught when I hear them say that."

"Thanks for your honesty, Daniel," Alex replied. "That is one of the things I have so appreciated about you through the years. The problem is, those are some amazing facts. Even if I don't believe them, or maybe the issue is that I don't *want* to believe them, facts are facts. One last question, Michael. If you have done all of this research and have all of these facts and even have them stored on your phone, why aren't you a believer?"

"Great question, Alex. Thanks for asking it. I am not sure. But if I had to be honest, it probably comes down to what I call pride and control. Once I am convinced there is a God and I answer to Him, then that means I am no longer the big dog in the hunt. I can't do what I want to do. Because once there is a God, He gets to set the standard and I do not. And you guys have always known that I want to be in control. The moment I don't think I am is a very difficult time for me. It is something I am wrestling with big time as I know my days are winding down."

Little does Josh know, but his day is winding down as well. He will cross the threshold of this life and step into eternity to meet the Messiah in just eight short hours.

7.

"**W**hy haven't we had these discussions before?" I wondered out loud. "This subject is so intriguing! Hey, what is that sign up ahead for the Punchbowl? Go ahead and get off here, Alex. That looks interesting. Since all of us used to enjoy those punch bowls at the dances back in the day, this will probably be something good for us to see!"

As we got out of our car, the place was so striking, and we knew that there was so much more here than just the beauty.

"Oh wow. This is a cemetery located in a volcanic crater. I have never seen anything like it. Let's pick up one of those brochures and see what it says."

NATIONAL MEMORIAL CEMETERY OF THE PACIFIC

Although there are various translations of the Punchbowl's Hawaiian name, "Puowaina," the most common is "Hill of Sacrifice." This translation closely relates to the history of the crater. The first known use was as an altar where Hawaiians offered human sacrifices to pagan gods, and they killed violators of the many taboos. Later, during the reign of Kamehameha the Great, a battery of two cannons was mounted at the rim of the crater to salute distinguished arrivals and signify important occasions. Early in the 1880s, leasehold land on the slopes of the Punchbowl opened for settlement, and in the 1930s, the crater was used as a rifle range for the Hawaii National Guard. Toward the end of World War II, tunnels were dug through the rim of the crater for the placement of shore batteries to guard Honolulu Harbor and the south edge of Pearl Harbor.

During the late 1890s, a committee recommended that the Punchbowl become the site for a new cemetery to accommodate the growing population of Honolulu. The idea was rejected for fear of polluting the water supply and the emotional aversion to creating a city of the dead above a city of the living.

Fifty years later, Congress authorized a small appropriation to establish a national cemetery in Honolulu with two provisions: that the location be acceptable to the War Department, and that the site would be donated rather than purchased. In 1943, the governor of Hawaii offered the Punchbowl for this purpose. The $50,000 appropriation proved insufficient, however, and the project was deferred until after World War II. By 1947, Congress and veteran organizations placed a great deal of pressure on the military to find a permanent burial site in Hawaii for the remains of thousands of World War II servicemen on the island of Guam awaiting permanent burial. Subsequently, the Army again began planning the Punchbowl cemetery; in February 1948 Congress approved funding and construction began.

Prior to the opening of the cemetery for the recently deceased, the remains of soldiers from locations around the Pacific Theater—including Wake Island and Japanese POW camps—were transported to Hawaii for final interment. The first interment was made Jan. 4, 1949. The cemetery opened to the public on July 19, 1949, with services for five war dead: an unknown serviceman, two Marines, an Army lieutenant and one civilian—noted war correspondent Ernie Pyle. Initially, the graves at National Memorial Cemetery of the Pacific were marked with white wooden crosses and Stars of David—like the American cemeteries abroad—in preparation for the dedication ceremony on the fourth anniversary of V-J Day. Eventually, over 13,000 soldiers and sailors who died during World War II would be laid to rest in the Punchbowl.

Despite the Army's extensive efforts to inform the public that the star- and cross-shaped grave markers were only temporary, an outcry arose in 1951 when permanent flat granite markers replaced them. A letter from the Quartermaster General to Senator Paul Douglas in December 1952 explained that while individual markers are inscribed according to the appropriate religious faith:

> *"Crosses do not mark the graves of the dead of our country in other national cemeteries. No cross marks the burial of our revered Unknown Soldier. From Arlington to Golden Gate, from Puerto Rico to Hawaii, the Government's markers in national cemeteries for all our hero-dead are of the traditional designs...[s]ome are upright and some are flat. None is in the form of a religious emblem."*

The National Memorial Cemetery of the Pacific was the first such cemetery to install Bicentennial Medal of Honor headstones, the medal insignia being defined in gold leaf. On May 11, 1976, a total of 23 of these were placed on the graves of medal recipients, all but one of whom were killed in action. The Punchbowl has become one of the area's most popular tourist destinations. More than five million visitors come to the cemetery each year to pay their respects to the dead and to enjoy the panoramic view from the Punchbowl. One of the most breathtaking views of the Island of Oahu can be found while standing at the highest point on the crater's rim.

In August 2001, about 70 generic unknown markers for the graves of men known to have died during the attack on Pearl Harbor were replaced with markers that included "USS Arizona" after it was determined they perished on this vessel. In addition, new information that identified grave locations of 175 men whose graves were previously marked as unknown resulted in the installation of new markers in October 2002. The National Memorial Cemetery of the Pacific was placed on the National Register of Historic Places in 1976.

MEMORIALS AND MONUMENTS

The National Memorial Cemetery of the Pacific contains a memorial pathway that is lined with a variety of memorials that honor America's veterans from various organizations. As of 2008, there were 56 such memorials throughout the National Memorial Cemetery of the Pacific—most commemorating soldiers of 20th century wars, including those killed at Pearl Harbor.[9]

"Oh, great! Here we are talking about lakes of fire, and now we are visiting the spot where they sacrificed people in a volcano! Why do I get the feeling that this is going to be a day to remember?" I said.

I'm reading in the Memorial's literature that this is the final resting place for over 25,000 soldiers who lost their lives in World War II, the Korean War, and the Vietnam War.

"Hey, let's walk up to that huge memorial and check it out. It looks beautiful in the distance."

The pamphlet for this memorial says:

THE MEMORIAL

The Honolulu Memorial was erected by the American Battle Monuments Commission in 1964 & was dedicated on May 1, 1966. It was erected to honor the sacrifices & achievements of American Armed Forces in the Pacific during World War II & the Korean Conflict. In 1980, it was enlarged to include the missing of the Vietnam Conflict.

The impressive memorial sits high on a wall of Puowaina Crater overlooking the graves area of the cemetery. It consists of a non-sectarian chapel, two map galleries, a monumental staircase leading from the crater floor to the Court Of Honor, ten Courts of the Missing & a Dedicatory Stone centered at the base of the stairway on which is inscribed:

IN THESE GARDENS ARE RECORDED THE
NAMES OF AMERICANS WHO GAVE THEIR LIVES IN
SERVICE TO THEIR COUNTRY AND WHOSE EARTHLY
RESTING PLACE IS KNOWN ONLY TO GOD

In the ten Courts of the Missing which flank the memorial staircase are recorded the names of 18,094 World War II heroes missing in action (MIA) or lost or buried at sea in the Pacific (excluding the Southwest Pacific & the Palau Islands - the MIAs from these areas are memorialized at the Manila American Cemetery), 8,195 in the Korea Conflict & 2,489 in the Vietnam Conflict, a total of 28,778 names.

On the front of the tower which houses the chapel is a 30-foot female figure, known as Columbia, standing on the symbolized prow of a U.S. Navy Carrier with a laurel branch in her left hand. Engraved below the figure is the poignant sympathy expressed by President Abraham Lincoln to Mrs. Bixby, mother of five sons who died in battle:

THE SOLEMN PRIDE THAT MUST BE YOURS
TO HAVE LAID SO COSTLY A SACRIFICE UPON
THE ALTAR OF FREEDOM.[10]

"Who is that lady?" I asked one of the men who was there.

He said, "That is Lady Columbia. Most people see her as a representation of all the mothers who have wept over the death of their children because of war. I am an 85-year-old WWII vet. I lost 17 buddies one time when a mortar round hit the chow line while we were in Europe. I am sure those moms wept over the loss of their sons. I am so glad that my mom didn't have to weep over me. But here I am at 85, and life goes by so, so fast. My two best friends now are Al and Art. Do you know them? Alzheimer and Arthritis are their full names! Not much time left for this old man."

As we walked away, Alex spoke up, "He was a funny man, but this is very sobering."

"Are you okay?" I asked.

"These memorials always get to me. It reminds me of my time in the military that was such a blessing. But we lost men from our company over in Iraq, and it is times like this when those memories come flooding back. You just love the guys that you work with; but when you are on the front lines, anything is possible."

"I noticed the silver band on your wrist, Alex. Is that for one of your soldiers?"

"We ran into a tough situation in Iraq. I lost a few of my men. That is the worst for a commanding officer. We had to finish the mission no matter how difficult it was. But when you are back at base, there are those long nights that you begin to think about those men and their families, and begin to wonder where they are right now?"

"Do those moments make you think about God and eternity?"

"Why don't we all sit down on the steps here and let me tell you a few things. Military folks have to think about life and death. It just goes with the territory. And when the men tell you they don't think about it, they are lying. You begin to contemplate things like, if there is a God why is He letting so much death take place? Why doesn't He just stop the whole thing? Is this all really worth it? But then you see some things out on the battlefield that you know there is no way you can explain in an earthly sense."

I replied, "Do you mean like God encounters or something like that?"

"There are just times out there that you really think, beyond a shadow of a doubt, that God, or one of His messengers, is in that battlefield with you."

Daniel said, "Why do I get the feeling you are going to send something to my phone?! I am kind of hoping my battery is going to die!"

"You know you are enjoying this conversation, Daniel. I can see it in your eyes, that it is making you think," I fired back in a nice way.

"If it is not too personal, can you relay some of those stories to us?" I continued.

"One thing soldiers do is talk. We communicate. We have to have open lines of communication in order to keep each other updated with what is going on. We need to know what we are doing and what the enemy is doing. It is just too important.

"But then we will also share things that sometimes you think we would keep to ourselves. But some events are so momentous and life-changing that you must tell others.

"You guys may have seen the movie *Black Hawk Down*, about when some of our Rangers were in Somalia. I actually got to talk to one of the men that was there on that mission. We were swapping ideas about how we could do things better here in the Army. He then related to me a fascinating encounter. He was in a Humvee going back into Mogadishu to get the body of one of our men who had been killed. We don't leave our guys behind. He said they were driving the Humvee at a high rate of speed through some very narrow alleyways. Now picture this, there is not much space between them and the walls, or the places where people live on each side. As they are traveling down this alleyway, all of a sudden, a guy steps out ahead of them with an RPG weapon. This is not good. There is no way he can miss them with that rocket-propelled grenade. He waits until they get closer. All of a sudden, the driver screams out, 'Jesus, don't let that grenade hit us!' Well, the guy shoots, and the grenade is heading straight for the hood of the car, but it rises up, goes over the hood and hits the wall on the other side! He related to me that every one of the guys in the Humvee knew that an angel or something protected them that day."

"I am glad that those guys are safe, Alex, but don't you believe in luck? That was just luck. Nothing more and nothing less. I am so glad they were lucky that day, but don't just throw that into the angelic realm," I said.

"I can see where you are coming from, Josh. But it is one of those things where you just have to be there. And the more you experience things like this and talk with the men who have had similar encounters, you are almost assured there is some unseen hand protecting you along the way.

"Some marines were telling me they were some of the first military to go into Iraq in 2003 at the beginning of Gulf War II. As they were approaching this area, a marine said that one of his fellow marines came up beside him. It was a big platoon, so he really didn't recognize the guy. Seemed familiar, but just wasn't sure. He said his name was Michael. He told the marine that there was trouble just up ahead. How did he know that? As they came around the corner, the bullets start flying. The marine dove to the ground and yelled at Michael to get down. He didn't. So the marine reached up to pull him down and was struck by a bullet. Then, he felt like someone was laying him on the ground with big, strong hands. He looked up, and it was Michael. All of a sudden, Michael's face transformed into this splendor that he couldn't describe. Wings came upon him, and he had this huge sword of fire. And then he was gone. He told me that people think he is crazy when he shares this story. His commanding officer told him later that he was amazed that he survived the firefight because he had strayed too far away from the team. When he mentioned Michael being there, the officer said, 'There are no Michaels in this platoon!'"

> *And he answered, Fear not: for they that be with us are more than they that be with them. And Elisha prayed, and said, LORD, I pray thee, open his eyes, that he may see. And the LORD opened the eyes of the young man; and he saw: and, behold, the mountain was full of horses and chariots of fire round about Elisha.* **2 Kings 6:16,17**

"If you guys have learned one thing in this lifetime, it is that you can trust anyone named Michael!" Michael responded.

"You have any more of those stories, Alex?" I said.

"Sure. One more to make you think. One of my guys was walking down a street. As he passed an open door about ten feet across the street from him, he heard some rustling. A man stepped out and six shots rang out. He said there was this glow or light in front of him. When the shooting stopped, the man who was doing the shooting ran back in the house and was gone. There was no way on earth he could have missed him. When my guy looked behind him, there were six bullet holes in the wall. Three on each side of him, evenly placed, all right above each other in perfect alignment. All he said was there had to be someone in front of him that was deflecting those bullets to each side so they would not hit him."

> *For he shall give his angels charge over thee, to keep thee in all thy ways. They shall bear thee up in their hands, lest thou dash thy foot against a stone.* **Psalm 91:11,12**

I piped in again at this point. "Well, Michael, we all know you are the research guy amongst this group, so I am assuming you have some stories as well, don't you?"

"Of course I do!" said Michael.

"Figures!"

"I was working on a young man one day who had broken his femur. His dad told me that he wanted to be with his son when he came out of the ICU. I saw his dad in the hallway, and he asked how his son was. I told him that he had already been released and was in his room. 'They didn't tell you?' Let's just say his dad was not too happy! He raced to get up to his son's room. When he walked in, he told his son that he was so sorry that he wasn't there when he came back to the room. His son replied, 'It is okay, dad. Uncle Jim was here when I got to the room.' 'Uncle Jim? We don't have an Uncle Jim, son.' 'Yes, dad. He was the guy in the brown suit that walked out of the room right before you walked in.' His dad went down the hall looking for this man and couldn't find him. He asked the nurses about this guy, and they said there was no guy in a brown suit on this floor. The man was flabbergasted by the encounter, but he told me that he knew it had to have been an angel."

Be not forgetful to entertain strangers: for thereby some have entertained angels unawares.   **Hebrews 13:2**

Daniel admitted, "That is powerful. But let me ask a question. If there are good angels, so to speak, doesn't that imply that there are bad angels as well?"

"You are tracking correctly, Daniel," Michael said. "There is actually a lot I haven't told you. So here goes. We had a patient one day who was not doing well, and he was going to die. He told one of the nurses, 'Do you see that demon in that chair waiting on me? Do you see him?' For twenty-four hours he kept talking about this demon that was sitting in this chair waiting for him. Right up until he died, he was still talking about this demon waiting for him, and wondering why none of us could see him."

"All right, Michael, you have me worried now. You know

you guys pump so many of us up on drugs, so that is all it was. He was hallucinating under the influence of those medications before he died," Daniel said.

"That is a possibility, Daniel, but there is so much more. That is one of the fun things about doing research. You just have no clue where it is going to take you.

"A teenager told me that he was very heavy into the drug culture. He became a Christian and decided to leave those drugs far behind. One day he was playing with incense in his garage. Some people will use incense to cover up the smell of drugs. All of a sudden, he said that the incense smoke began to bubble up. A head started forming out of the smoke! He then said that these red piercing eyes appeared in that head. Then the smoke began to form into arms and then hands at the end of the arms. He said that the demon—and he knew it was a demon—grabbed him by the throat and flung him against the garage door. If that wasn't enough, the demon spoke to him! The demon said, 'I am not going to let you go easy.'"

For we wrestle not against flesh and blood, but against principalities, against powers, against the rulers of the darkness of this world, against spiritual wickedness in high places. **Ephesians 6:12**

"Another teenager told me that he was driving his car one time. He ran off the side of the road. The car flipped three times. He told me that when he 'came to' that he wasn't sure if he was alive or dead. He just didn't know. He said there were all these black-winged creatures all around him. They all had these red, piercing eyes. And all he could feel was this evil around him. He then said this bright bolt of light came out of nowhere. When it hit where the demons were, they instantly scattered and were gone. He was alive here on earth and was so, so thankful.

"Another teen also told me one day that a demon was appearing in his bedroom. It would appear at his bedroom door and would begin to walk towards his bed. As the demon, with a long black trench coat, red piercing eyes, and black top hat, walked towards him, he said that he felt like there was a cement block that was pinning him to the bed, and he couldn't move. He said the demon would just stand there and stare at him. After a short while, it would turn and exit out of the bathroom. There was only one problem. He lived on the second floor of his house. There was not an exit there! Well, his girlfriend told him one time that if it happened again, to follow him to the bathroom and see where he goes. And that is one reason we have to tell our kids to be very careful who they date! Well, the demon appeared again. The same scenario occurred. So he decided to follow the demon to the bathroom. After the demon had disappeared, he got up and followed. As he approached the bathroom, he told me that all of a sudden the demon whipped his head around the corner and spoke to him! It said in a very gravelly voice, 'Don't you ever follow me again.' So, I asked the teenager what he did then. He said that he flew back into his bed and got under the covers! Sounds like a good move to me!

"But that wasn't the end of the story. His father ended up taking him to a spiritual warfare expert to see if they could figure out what was going on. The expert asked the teen to draw out this demon. As he drew him and presented the picture to the expert, he told me the expert said, 'I know who this is. This demon is appearing to at least six different people that I know of right now across America.' Well, let's just say the teen and his dad were a little shocked by that!"

Be sober, be vigilant; because your adversary the devil, as a roaring lion, walketh about, seeking whom he may devour: **1 Peter 5:8**

Michael continued, "I was with my kids in a mall one day and saw these two people in kind of dark, gothic-looking clothing with safety pins all stuck in their leather coats. They looked interesting, so I went over to chat with them. I have always enjoyed meeting people, and you can learn the neatest things just by talking with folks. As I have always said, 'Everyone has a story.' But sometimes we are just too busy, and we walk right on by people who have a story to tell. They told me that they were into black magic. So as we talked back and forth, they explained to me that it wasn't white magic, which would be something like Wicca. Black magic was the harder form of magic. Now that got me interested, because they said that both of those connected into the demonic side of our universe. Well, if it is black magic or white magic, and it is connecting to demons, I am not sure that is something that we should be playing around with! They then said that they would pray to Satan and do incantations, and sometimes demons would appear to them. They claimed that there were good and bad demons. Now, I am just a medical doctor and not a rocket scientist, but a demon is a demon! You don't want to mess with them. They continued and told me that you could tell if it was a good demon or a bad demon by how many stripes were on its heel. Sounded a bit strange to me, but their faces were telling me that this was a real experience. They told me that sometimes the demon would speak, and one time it said, 'Right now I have power over you, but when you die you will have power over me in hell.'"

Ye are of your father the devil, and the lusts of your father ye will do. He was a murderer from the beginning, and abode not in the truth, because there is no truth in him. When he speaketh a lie, he speaketh of his own: for he is a liar, and the father of it. **John 8:44**

Michael said, "This isn't a game, guys. You should see these people's faces. Football is a game. Basketball is a game, but these demonic encounters are not. It is serious business.

He continued, "I was vacationing in St. Augustine, Florida, one time, and it started to rain a bit. I thought it was going to pour, and I ended up being right. I saw this long-haired guy walking along the side of the road. I said, 'Do you need a ride?' He did, so he hopped in my car. As I was driving, I noticed a tattoo on his arm, and I asked him what that was. He told me that it was a pentagram. So I asked him why he put a pentagram, or a five pointed star, on himself. He said he was thinking about getting into Satanism, but hadn't done it yet. I am thinking in my head, 'Why did you get the tattoo?!! Wouldn't you wait until you joined the Satanists before you got it?' You guys know I have always been a little crazy, so I asked, 'Why haven't you joined them yet?' And he gave me one of the most interesting answers that I have ever heard in my life. He said, 'Well, if I would choose to believe in Satan, then I would have to believe in the Bible because that is where Satan came from. But if I believed in the Bible, then I might as well believe in God since He is much more powerful than Satan could ever be!' I have always loved logical people, and this guy was sure being logical."

God hath spoken once; twice have I heard this; that power belongeth unto God.   **Psalm 62:11**

Daniel chimed in, "Most of these encounters you are telling us, Michael, are from teens. We have all had teens in our homes, and you know they can exaggerate and embellish just a little bit, or maybe even a lot a bit!"

"That is good thinking, Daniel. But I am not finished. A friend of mine does some prison ministry work," Michael continued. "He told me that he was in a prison one day talking to some prisoners. He saw a big group of inmates praying on the football field. He told the guys that it was good to see people praying. A prisoner responded, 'Here at this prison, you really want to find out who they are praying to!' So my friend asked the prisoner to go and find out. When he came back, he stated that they were praying all right. They were praying to Satan. Well, that got my friend's intrigue up, so he walked over that way later. As my friend began talking with this one man, he began to relay a very interesting story. One day, the man said, he was praying to Satan, and all of a sudden, Satan appeared to him down a long corridor or hallway at the prison. He stated he was sure that it was not a demon but Lucifer himself. So my friend asked him to describe him. He said Lucifer was this absolutely beautiful being with long flowing hair who looked like an angel of light."

And no marvel; for Satan himself is transformed into an angel of light. **2 Corinthians 11:14**

"He said that as he looked at this being, all he wanted was more, and more, and more. That really got me thinking. That is what sin does. You have a drink, and you want another, and another, and another. People on drugs want more, and more, and more. People who sleep around want to do it again, and again, and again. I have seen this so many times in the emergency room. It was people's lust for something that seemed to be what destroyed them."

Let not sin therefore reign in your mortal body, that ye should obey it in the lusts thereof. **Romans 6:12**

"On a trip to Gatlinburg, Tennessee, one time with the family, I was walking the streets and saw this man with a very dark, gothic-looking T-shirt on. So I just went up and chatted with him. The shirt was for a heavy metal band that he liked. He then relayed an encounter that happened to him one time. He said he was lying in bed listening to this genre of music that he loved. He told me that Lucifer appeared in front of his bed! He was stunned. I asked what happened. He said that Lucifer stood there and just laughed at him. There was this mocking tone to his laughter. He said he spoke to Lucifer and asked why he was laughing at him. He said Lucifer spoke to him! He said, 'Because of all that anti-Jesus music you listen to.' And as I looked more closely at his T-shirt, it was mocking the resurrection of Jesus. You fellas should have seen the countenance on this guy's face. It was no joke. It was a real experience, and he had a frightful look on his face as he had to relive that encounter once again."

How art thou fallen from heaven, O Lucifer, son of the morning! how art thou cut down to the ground, which didst weaken the nations!   **Isaiah 14:12**

"Giving a lecture at Clemson one time, a student came up to me to chat afterwards. She told me that once she had died on her couch. Since I work in emergency rooms, I wanted to know how she knew that. She told me that her soul exited her body and was hovering in the room above her body on the couch. I have heard that from people before in the emergency room, that as I was paddling them trying to get them to come back, they were hovering above the operating table staring down at what I was doing and seeing their body still lying there! The college student said that as she was hovering above her body, this cold, evil presence began to surround her. It was very intense and very scary. She then said all she could hear was this evil, hissing laughter. She said to me, 'Sir, what must I do to make sure I never hear that laughter again?' Sadly, I had no answer for her. But as she relayed this story to me, I knew that encounter had scared her very, very much."

And that they may recover themselves out of the snare of the devil, who are taken captive by him at his will.   **2 Timothy 2:26**

"As I was chatting with one of my daughters one day, I had her take out a piece of paper to write something down for me. I asked her this question: What did she think her friends were doing or were into that she thought could be evil or could affect their lives in a bad way? Let me read her list to you:

1. Pornography

"She said this was very big with both the boys and the girls at school."

2. Music

"Remember that we would listen to 'Imagine' by John Lennon which says, 'Imagine there's no heaven/It's easy if you try/No hell below us/Above us only sky'? She told me that one of the kids' favorite songs 'Breakeven' had the lyric, 'Just prayed to a God that I don't believe in.' You begin to wonder how much of an impact these songs have on us."

3. Role playing games like Dungeons and Dragons or Masquerade

"During my vacation to St. Augustine, I was talking with some people on the boardwalk that were living out the vampire lifestyle. I asked them how they got into it. They told me that they got into the role-playing game Masquerade and decided to actually live it out!"

4. Drinking

"Do you guys remember as kids when just about all liquor stores used to be called Wine and Spirits? I wonder if we were messing with spirits by doing that. Remember when our parents would say things like there is a 'demon in that bottle.' So many people I know would have a complete change of character when they were drinking, and, of course, it usually wasn't for the good. We saw the effects of that way too much in the emergency room."

5. Drugs

"My daughter was stunned at how many drugs her friends were using. And it wasn't just the illegal ones. At some parties, the kids would come in with a couple of bottles of their parents' prescription medication. They would dump them into a big bowl and mix them up. Then they would reach in and take two or more of the pills and swallow them. She told me that some of the friends would have some very bad reactions just trying to find that elusive high."

Daniel broke in, "When my daughter was at Diablo, she was in the drama department. She said some really weird things began to happen. There were a lot of New Age things going on. She said that as she worked on certain projects, it almost seemed like she wasn't doing the acting, but someone was doing it through her. She even found a quote from a famous actress who said that once she 'almost felt like the spirit of that person took over my body to play that person.' She also told me that some of the students had gotten into astral projection, out-of-body experiences, and spirit-guided journeys. It intrigued me a bit, so I began to ask her some questions. She said one of the girls could actually push her soul out of her body and then go on these journeys to the other side. I know that sounds weird, fellas, but she said it was commonplace in some of these circles. They could actually choose a spirit guide, so this girl had chosen Jesus since she grew up in a Christian home. Now, you know I don't believe in any of that, but it sure had my daughter thinking. Another girl in the group was one of those 'born again' Christians, and she didn't play with all of this stuff. So she told the other girl that it was not the Jesus of the Bible, and if she ever decided to do that again, to ask the spirit guide if he is the Jesus of the Bible. The girl decided to take another one of those journeys. When her spirit guide met her, she asked him if he was the Jesus of the Bible. She said that this 'Jesus' figure looked at her and just stared. Then all of a sudden, his face began to crack down the middle, and a werewolf head popped out snarling at her! Her friend knew instantly that it was a demon and never took one of those journeys ever again."

I spoke up and said, "That is crazy. If that is true, I never want to see anything like that. I had a co-worker tell me a story one day. His mom was dying, so he went to the hospital. He told me that he and his wife were there. He is a very strong Christian. So, he began to talk with his mom again about Jesus. He said that she looked at him and said, 'Honey, you can choose your Jesus. I am going to choose my good works.' He said that all of a sudden, her eyes opened huge as she was seeing something. She kept screaming, but no sound came out of her mouth. She died three different times. Every time they brought her back, she had the same eyes and the same wide open mouth screaming with nothing coming out. He told me that she had this beautiful white skin. Just gorgeous. All of a sudden, it became gray and wrinkly as she took her last breath and died."

"One of my daughters went to a summer camp. She said that some of the boys told her a crazy story one day. They were in their room when, all of a sudden, the bathroom door opened up when it had been closed. They all felt this cool breeze in the room. So one of them got up and closed the door. It happened a second time. The boy got up and closed the door again. It happened a third time! They knew it was something out of the realm of what they had been accustomed to. They all hit their knees and began to pray! Then one of the boys remembered that he made the comment earlier that morning, 'I think it would be really cool to see a demon sometime.' He got his wish, but it wasn't a good wish."

"Michael, you have really added a lot to the knowledge I already had on the subject of angels and demons. Thank you," Alex said and then continued, "But all that I found out about angels and demons really had me thinking about the supernatural, and if heaven and hell really do exist. Then something happened with my wife. When we had our first child, there were a bunch of new mothers in the neighborhood. They all kind of made up a group that shared parenting tips, etc. Most of the ladies were evangelical Christians, and, of course, we are Catholic. After a while, I noticed that my wife was doing a lot of Bible reading, so I began to ask her some questions. She ended up telling me that after one of her encounters with the ladies, she had become a Christian. I noticed some wonderful changes in her even though she was wonderful already. It made me do some soul-searching. One thing she kept telling me was to keep looking at the Bible as the standard and to compare things to that book. Well, that sent me into research mode. I wanted to find out more about Catholicism since that is our tradition. You can't get any more Catholic than Notre Dame! I needed to know the official teachings of the Catholic Church. If I knew those, then I could figure things out. So I went to the Catholic Catechism of 1994, which has the imprimatur of the Catholic Church and was made official by John Paul II. I found out some very interesting things about Roman Catholicism. Okay, I think you know what I am going to say; check your phones!

"As we go through this, you'll see the teaching of the Roman Catholic Church with paragraph numbers. Then it will have some Scripture verses that my wife wanted me to look at. Then at different points, you will see some questions and comments that I put in bold."

ROMAN CATHOLICISM COMPARED TO THE BIBLE

The largest religious denomination in the United States is the Roman Catholic Church. Between 60-70 million people consider themselves Roman Catholic, which is a little over 20% of the American population. To find out the official position of the Catholic Church, all you have to do is look at its official positions which are written down in the Catechism of the Catholic Church. The text was approved by Pope John Paul II in 1992. It is broken down into paragraph numbers signified by the # symbol.

#97 "Sacred Tradition and Sacred Scripture make up a single sacred deposit of the Word of God..."	**Colossians 2:8** "Beware lest any man spoil you through philosophy and vain deceit, after the tradition of men, after the rudiments of the world, and not after Christ."

Is it the Bible alone for truth or the Bible plus the traditions of men?

#181 "'Believing' is an ecclesial act. The Church's faith precedes, engenders, supports and nourishes our faith. The Church is the mother of all believers. 'No one can have God as Father who does not have the Church as Mother.'"	**John 6:44-46** "No man can come to me, except the Father which hath sent me draw him: and I will raise him up at the last day. It is written in the prophets, And they shall be all taught of God. Every man therefore that hath heard, and hath learned of the Father, cometh unto me. Not that any man hath seen the Father, save he which is of God, he hath seen the Father."
#868 "The Church is catholic: she proclaims the fullness of the faith. She bears in herself and administers the totality of the means of salvation. She is sent out to all peoples. She speaks to all men. She encompasses all times. She is 'missionary of her' very nature."	**Acts 4:12** "Neither is there salvation in any other: for there is none other name under heaven given among men, whereby we must be saved."
#1461 "Since Christ entrusted to his apostles the ministry of reconciliation, bishops who are their successors, and priests, the bishops' collaborators, continue to exercise this ministry. Indeed bishops and priests, by virtue of the sacrament of Holy Orders,	**Matthew 9:6** "But that ye may know that the Son of man hath power on earth to forgive sins, (then saith he to the sick of the palsy,) Arise, take up thy bed, and go unto thine house."

| have the power to forgive all sins 'in the name of the Father, and of the Son, and of the Holy Spirit.'" | **Mark 2:7** "Why doth this man thus speak blasphemies? who can forgive sins but God only?" |

Do I need to belong to the Catholic Church for salvation, or is it enough just to go through Jesus alone?

| **#1257** "The Lord himself affirms that Baptism is necessary for salvation. He also commands his disciples to proclaim the Gospel to all nations and to baptize them. Baptism is necessary for salvation for those to whom the Gospel has been proclaimed and who have had the possibility of asking for this sacrament. The Church does not know of any means other than Baptism that assures entry into eternal beatitude; this is why she takes care not to neglect the mission she has received from the Lord to see that all who can be baptized are 'reborn of water and the Spirit.' God has bound salvation to the sacrament of Baptism, but he himself is not bound by his sacraments." | **Romans 10:9-13** "That if thou shalt confess with thy mouth the Lord Jesus, and shalt believe in thine heart that God hath raised him from the dead, thou shalt be saved. For with the heart man believeth unto righteousness; and with the mouth confession is made unto salvation. For the scripture saith, Whosoever believeth on him shall not be ashamed. For there is no difference between the Jew and the Greek: for the same Lord over all is rich unto all that call upon him. For whosoever shall call upon the name of the Lord shall be saved. How then shall they call on him in whom they have not believed? and how shall they believe in him of whom they have not heard? and how shall they hear without a preacher?"

1 Corinthians 1:17 "For Christ sent me not to baptize, but to preach the gospel: not with wisdom of words, lest the cross of Christ should be made of none effect." |

Baptism or Jesus for salvation?

88

#1374 "The mode of Christ's presence under the Eucharistic species is unique. It raises the Eucharist above all the sacraments as 'the perfection of the spiritual life and the end to which all the sacraments tend.' In the most blessed sacrament of the Eucharist 'the body and blood, together with the soul and divinity, of our Lord Jesus Christ and, therefore, the whole Christ is truly, really and substantially contained.' 'This presence is called 'real' too, but because it is presence in the fullest sense: that is to say, it is a substantial presence by which Christ, God and man, makes himself wholly and entirely present.'"

Luke 22:14-19 "And when the hour was come, he sat down, and the twelve apostles with him. And he said unto them, With desire I have desired to eat this passover with you before I suffer: For I say unto you, I will not any more eat thereof, until it be fulfilled in the kingdom of God. And he took the cup, and gave thanks, and said, Take this, and divide it among yourselves: For I say unto you, I will not drink of the fruit of the vine, until the king- dom of God shall come. And he took bread, and gave thanks, and brake it, and gave unto them, saying, This is my body which is given for you: this do in remembrance of me."

How can the Eucharist be Jesus when He says to do this 'in remembrance of Me'?

#1393 "Holy Communion separates us from sin. The body of Christ we receive in Holy Communion is 'given up for us,' and the blood we drink 'shed for the many for the forgiveness of sins.' For this reason the Eucharist cannot unite us to Christ without at the same time cleansing us from past sins and preserving us from future sins: For as often as we eat this bread and drink

1 John 1:7 "But if we walk in the light, as he is in the light, we have fellowship one with another, and the blood of Jesus Christ his Son cleanseth us from all sin."

1 John 2:2 "And he is the propitiation for our sins: and not for ours only, but also for the sins of the whole world."

the cup, we proclaim the death of the Lord. If we proclaim the Lord's death, we proclaim the forgiveness of sins. If, as often as his blood is poured out, it is poured for the forgiveness of sins, I should always receive it, so that it may always forgive my sins. Because I always sin, I should always have a remedy."

Acts 13:38,39 "Be it known unto you therefore, men and brethren, that through this man is preached unto you the forgiveness of sins: And by him all that believe are justified from all things, from which ye could not be justified by the law of Moses."

By taking the bread and wine, will that really get rid of my sins?

#841 "The Church's relationship with the Muslims. 'The plan of salvation also includes those who acknowledge the Creator, in the first place amongst whom are the Muslims; these profess to hold the faith of Abraham, and together with us they adore the one, merciful God, mankind's judge on the last day.'"

John 3:36 "He that believeth on the Son hath everlasting life: and he that believeth not the Son shall not see life; but the wrath of God abideth on him."

Romans 9:7 "Neither, because they are the seed of Abraham, are they all children: but, In Isaac shall thy seed be called."

How can a Muslim get to heaven when they do not believe Jesus is the Son of God who died for their sins?

#1030, 1031 "All who die in God's grace and friendship, but still imperfectly purified, are indeed assured of their eternal salvation; but after death they undergo purification, so as to achieve the holiness necessary to enter the joy of heaven. The Church gives the name Purgatory to this final purification of the elect, which is entirely different from the

John 19:30 "When Jesus therefore had received the vinegar, he said, It is finished: and he bowed his head, and gave up the ghost."

1 John 4:10 "Herein is love, not that we loved God, but that he loved us, and sent his Son to be the propitiation for our sins."

punishment of the damned. The Church formulated her doctrine of faith on Purgatory especially: at the Councils of Florence and Trent. The tradition of the Church, by reference to certain texts of Scripture, speaks of a cleansing fire:"	**2 Corinthians 5:8** "We are confident, I say, and willing rather to be absent from the body, and to be present with the Lord." **Hebrews 10:17** "And their sins and iniquities will I remember no more."

Purgatory isn't in the Bible!

#969 "This motherhood of Mary in the order of grace continues uninterruptedly from the consent which she loyally gave at the Annunciation and which she sustained without wavering beneath the cross, until the eternal fulfillment of all the elect. Taken up to heaven she did not lay aside this saving office but by her manifold intercession continues to bring us the gifts of eternal salvation... Therefore the Blessed Virgin is invoked in the Church under the titles of Advocate, Helper, Benefactress, and Mediatrix."	**Luke 1:46,47** "And Mary said, My soul doth magnify the Lord, And my spirit hath rejoiced in God my Saviour." **1 Timothy 2:5** "For there is one God, and one mediator between God and men, the man Christ Jesus;" **1 John 2:1** "My little children, these things write I unto you, that ye sin not. And if any man sin, we have an advocate with the Father, Jesus Christ the righteous:"

Is Jesus my Advocate to get to God, or is it Mary?

#460 "The Word became flesh to make us 'partakers of the divine nature': 'For this is why the Word became man, and the Son of God became the Son of man: so that man, by entering into communion with the Word and thus receiving divine sonship, might	**Genesis 3:5** "For God doth know that in the day ye eat thereof, then your eyes shall be opened, and ye shall be as gods, knowing good and evil."

become a son of God.' 'For the Son of God became man so that we might become God.' 'The only-begotten Son of God, wanting to make us sharers in his divinity, assumed our nature, so that he, made man, might make men gods.'"

Isaiah 45:5 "I am the Lord, and there is none else, there is no God beside me: I girded thee, though thou has not known me:"

I can become a god? I don't think so! I think I will stick with Whoever made this universe!

#846 "How are we to understand this affirmation, often repeated by the Church Fathers? Re-formulated positively, it means that all salvation comes from Christ the Head through the Church which is his Body: 'Basing itself on Scripture and Tradition, the Council teaches that the Church, a pilgrim now on earth, is necessary for salvation: the one Christ is the mediator and the way of salvation; he is present to us in his body which is the Church. He himself explicitly asserted the necessity of faith and Baptism, and thereby affirmed at the same time the necessity of the Church which men enter through Baptism as through a door. Hence they could not be saved who, knowing that the Catholic Church was founded as necessary by God through Christ, would refuse either to enter it or to remain in it.'"

John 14:6 "Jesus saith unto him, I am the way, the truth and the life: no man cometh unto the Father, but by me."

Romans 1:16 "For I am not ashamed of the gospel of Christ: for it is the power of God unto salvation to every one that believeth; to the Jew first, and also to the Greek."

Ephesians 1:13 "In whom ye also trusted, after that ye heard the word of truth, the gospel of your salvation: in whom also after that ye believed, ye were sealed with that Holy Spirit of promise,"

So if someone leaves the Catholic Church, they can't get to heaven?

What about the tons of people who have left and still believe in Jesus for the forgiveness of their sins??

WHERE ARE YOU GOING TO SPEND ETERNITY?

you can be saved right now! It's now up to you! Just bow your head and pray to God in your own words, and admit to Him that you are a guilty sinner who deserves hell, but that with all your heart, you believe Jesus Christ can save you from hell and change your way of life. The Bible says, *"That if thou shalt confess with thy mouth the Lord Jesus, and shalt believe in thine heart that God hath raised him from the dead, thou shalt be saved...For whosoever shall call upon the name of the Lord shall be saved."* (Romans 10:9, 13)

If you have chosen not to admit your guilt and to trust Jesus Christ as your Saviour, please read what the Bible says *"...he that believeth not is condemned already, because he hath not believed in the name of the only begotten Son of God."* (John 3:18) Please don't reject the Gospel! Trust Christ today!

If you have decided to trust Jesus Christ as your Saviour after reading this tract, please write and let us know.

Name _____

Address _____

City _____ Zip _____

State _____ Age _____

Haven of Rest Baptist Church
320 Campbell Avenue
West Haven, CT 06516
203-934-6714 / horbc.org

FELLOWSHIP TRACT LEAGUE
P.O. BOX 164 • LEBANON, OH 45036
www.fellowshiptractleague.org © Tract 130
All tracts free as the Lord provides. Not to be sold.

Alex said, "You guys remember the grotto at Notre Dame, don't you? I always found it so interesting and yet so strange that people would pray to Mary and light candles in there. I kept wondering, why don't you go straight to God with those prayers? Something didn't seem right.

"During my research, I even talked with six bishops of the church. I asked each one of them what it took to get to heaven. I got the same answer from each one of them: I either had to do good works to get there, or belong to the Roman Catholic Church, or do both to enter heaven when I die.

"So as you can see, I had a dilemma." Alex continued, "I was grounded in Catholic schools. We all went to Notre Dame. Notre Dame means 'Our Lady.' So is she the redeemer of our sins, or is Jesus? Can the Eucharist or the priest forgive us of our sins, or does Jesus? Is the Bible plus tradition what we need to know, or is it the Bible alone? Can we actually become gods as the Catechism states? Do Muslims go to heaven because they are sincere, or do they need to go through Jesus? I was left with so, so many questions. None of these teachings were in the Bible like my wife was showing me. So I decided to walk away from the church. Now, I didn't become one of those evangelicals or anything like that, but there were just too many questions and not enough answers for me. I guess you can call me one of those lapsed Catholics.

"My wife said something very interesting one time, that the word 'deceived' shows up 73 times in the Bible. She even said Satan is known as the Great Deceiver. All I know is that I don't want to be deceived by anyone, and I especially don't want to be deceived about eternity."

And Jesus answered and said unto them, Take heed that no man deceive you. **Matthew 24:4**

And the great dragon was cast out, that old serpent, called the Devil, and Satan, which deceiveth the whole world: he was cast out into the earth, and his angels were cast out with him. **Revelation 12:9**

"You sure did a lot of research, Alex! I get the feeling none of us will ever forget this trip to the Punchbowl! Let's head back to Waikiki," I said.

Josh doesn't realize that his eternal clock is ticking, and he will soon enter eternity, just like all of these soldiers at the Punchbowl, in just a few short hours.

6.

"**N**ow that we are finally back at the hotel, some of you guys look like you need a nap! I guess that jet lag and old age are getting to you! What time should we meet for dinner, Michael?"

"Five o'clock in the lobby. I have something special for you guys tonight!"

As I headed down the hallway to my room, I noticed the cleaning lady's cart outside my door. Looks like no nap for me! But that is okay, because it is my 50th birthday, and I have no plans to waste any part of this day at all! As I walked up to the door, I could hear some beautiful singing—and I do mean beautiful!

"Hey, how are you?"

"Oh, I am sorry, sir. I will be done with your room in just a minute."

"What is your name?"

"Shaniqua. My momma loved that name, and that is what she named me!"

"My name is Josh. Okay, here is my question. Where did you get that beautiful voice?"

"Oh, that is very kind of you. I do love to sing."

"Can you please sing that song you were singing when I walked in?"

"Are you serious?"

"You bet I am."

"Well, I probably shouldn't do that."

"It is my birthday and a special one at that. Could it be my birthday gift to hear you sing that song again?"

"Well, you have me on that one. I love birthdays. Happy birthday and here goes!"

He Lives

I serve a risen Saviour,
He's in the world today;
I know that He is living,
Whatever men may say;
I see His hand of mercy,
I hear His voice of cheer,
And just the time I need Him
He's always near.

(Chorus)
He lives, He lives, Christ Jesus lives today!
He walks with me and He talks with me
Along life's narrow way.
He lives, He lives, salvation to impart!
You ask me how I know He lives:
He lives within my heart.

In all the world around me
I see His loving care,
And tho my heart grows weary
I never will despair;
I know that He is leading
Thro' all the stormy blast,
The day of His appearing
Will come at last.

(Chorus)

Rejoice, rejoice, O Christian,
Lift up your voice and sing
Eternal hallelujahs
To Jesus Christ the King!
The hope of all who seek Him,
The help of all who find,
None other is so loving,
So good and kind.

(Chorus)[11]

"What an elegant voice you have! It is almost angelic. Where did you learn that song?"

"You seem like a smart man, Josh. Do you know where Whitney Houston got her gorgeous voice?"

"Actually, I do. I was reading something about her, and she got that voice singing in a gospel choir."

"Right on, Josh. You see, one thing you learn about black folk, especially from the South, is that we grow up in church. Now we may not stay in it, we may even stray many miles from the truths of God, but it is very, very foundational for black people to grow up in a church. I was in church whenever the doors were open. A couple of times on Sunday, and Wednesday for sure, and even some other times during the week, as well. Momma always wanted me singing in the church choir, and that is what I did!"

"Well, your mom made a great decision."

"Did you not grow up in church, Josh?"

"Well, we were kind of the Christmas- and Easter-type of churchgoers. So, I guess it was more traditions and things like that with our family. My parents taught me to brush my teeth, tie my shoes, eat my vegetables, and what sports team to cheer for, but they didn't teach me much about God. They were just kind of like 'you can decide for yourself on the religion thing.'"

"That is not good, Josh. If you are not serious about God and Jesus, you are pretty much wasting your life. What did you do on New Year's Eve last year?"

"That is a strange question that came out of nowhere!"

"Trust me, Josh, I am going somewhere with it."

"We had a big get-together at our house in Chicago. Had a few families over, and just kind of celebrated and partied. Okay, where are you going with this?"

"Let me give you a little history lesson here, Josh. Don't worry, I am not going to charge you for it. Do you have a phone, Josh?"

"I can't believe this, but I know exactly where this is going! Yes, here is my number, so send me what you want to send me."

"You make me laugh, Josh! This is something you can keep for a very long time. Okay, here you go."

WATCH NIGHT

Although New Year's Eve church services were started in the mid-1700s by John Wesley, founder of the Methodist movement, the event, known as Watch Night, occupies a special place in black communities across America.

In 1863, when President Abraham Lincoln announced that the Emancipation Proclamation would take effect January 1, freeing all slaves in Confederate states, abolitionists and slaves reportedly gathered together on what was called "Freedom's Eve" to await and watch what the new year would bring.

This act would eventually become known as Watch Night. Many black churches even continue the tradition of reading the Emancipation Proclamation during the ceremony.[12]

"I am in church every New Year's Eve. It holds special meaning for us black people, who were hoping that this was the year slavery was going to end. And it was! So we commemorate that and thank God for ending those dark days for us. We also want to be prepared for the coming year. So we pray, we read the Word of God, and praise Him in song, all in anticipation of the coming year."

"Now hold up, Shaniqua. If you believe in God, why do you think He allowed all of that slavery?"

"You're a funny man, Josh. But I can already tell I like you! God gives people free will, Josh. We are not robots. We all have a conscience, and we can use that free will to have a wonderful conversation like we are having, or we can use that free will to do evil and wicked things.

"Do you have a porch at your house, Josh?"

"You ask the most interesting questions. No, it's a town-house."

"Well, you need to get you a porch and soon! In Hawaii it is called a *lanai*. We used to sit on that porch when we were young and talk about the things of God for hours on end. I am talking hours! We would get our sweet tea—I hope you know what that is, Josh!—and talk about the Bible, God, Jesus, salvation, heaven and hell, and other things. Those were the best afternoons! We learned so much in those days, and the good thing when you talk about God, is that everyone has an opinion!"

"Since you asked me a question out of the blue, I am going to ask you one."

"Go right ahead."

"Why do so many black women have abortions?"

"Ahh, you are hitting close to home, but that is a fair question. I know there is a reason you are asking it, but I won't ask why. I am going to assume that you don't read the Bible, do you, Josh?"

"No, I don't."

"If you look right here in this drawer, we have one for you! And it is for people just like you. This book has the words of eternal life. All you need to do is read it and study it, and you will find that out. But one thing you see when you read this book is that there is not just a God, but there is a Satan as well. God has an archenemy who hates Him and hates the people created in His image. Don't forget, Josh, that people are the best, of the best, of the best of what God has made. Even though we do some crazy things at times and can treat others horribly, there is nothing more special to God than people made in His image."

And God said, Let us make man in our image, after our likeness: and let them have dominion over the fish of the sea, and over the fowl of the air, and over the cattle, and over all the earth, and over every creeping thing that creepeth upon the earth. So God created man in his own image, in the image of God created he him; male and female created he them. **Genesis 1:26,27**

"You see, Josh, that Satan has a plan. He comes to steal, kill, and destroy."

The thief cometh not, but for to steal, and to kill, and to destroy: I am come that they might have life, and that they might have it more abundantly. **John 10:10**

"He has always been a murderer and always will be."

Ye are of your father the devil, and the lusts of your father ye will do. He was a murderer from the beginning, and abode not in the truth, because there is no truth in him. When he speaketh a lie, he speaketh of his own: for he is a liar, and the father of it. **John 8:44**

"He loves destroying human life. Why? Because people are made in the image of God, and that's one way he tries to get back at God. He has completely deceived our community. We kill so many of our little boys and girls. It is outrageous. We have killed so many black doctors, lawyers, scientists, teachers, moms, and dads. It is really a very sad blight on our community."

"You really believe that?"

"Oh, yes, I do. I know what the Word of God says, and that is what I live by. I am not ashamed of that one bit."

"Another question for you, Shaniqua. Was Jesus black or white?"

"You are a funny man, Josh! But I do like you. Now look at me. Here I am a pretty black woman! Okay, not everyone has that opinion, but I do. Do you think I care one bit if He was black or white? I care about one thing, Josh: Can His blood wash me clean of all my sins? If He can do that, I don't care what color He is. I just want to give Him a big hug and a big 'thank you' when I finally get to see Him!!"

100

But if we walk in the light, as he is in the light, we have fellowship one with another, and the blood of Jesus Christ his Son cleanseth us from all sin.   1 John 1:7

"Did I tell you it is my birthday?"

"Of course, you did!"

"How about one more song for me? I know you have another one in you!"

"If it wasn't your birthday, no way. But I love birthdays! Here goes."

The Old Rugged Cross

On a hill far away stood an old rugged cross,
The emblem of suffering and shame;
And I love that old cross where the dearest and best
For a world of lost sinners was slain.

Refrain:
So I'll cherish the old rugged cross,
Till my trophies at last I lay down;
I will cling to the old rugged cross,
And exchange it some day for a crown.

O that old rugged cross, so despised by the world,
Has a wondrous attraction for me;
For the dear Lamb of God left his glory above
To bear it to dark Calvary.

(Refrain)

In that old rugged cross, stained with blood so divine,
A wondrous beauty I see,
For 'twas on that old cross Jesus suffered and died,
To pardon and sanctify me.

(Refrain)

To that old rugged cross I will ever be true,
Its shame and reproach gladly bear;
Then he'll call me some day to my home far away,
Where his glory forever I'll share.

(Refrain)[13]

"When does your CD come out? I will stand in line to get it!"

"You are a funny guy, aren't you, Uncle Josh?"

"Uncle Josh?"

"That is a term of endearment or a sign of respect here on the Islands. We will say, 'Uncle so and so,' or 'Auntie so and so.'"

"You really do love Jesus, don't you, Auntie Shaniqua?"

For I am not ashamed of the gospel of Christ: for it is the power of God unto salvation to every one that believeth; to the Jew first, and also to the Greek. **Romans 1:16**

"You make me smile, Josh! I could not even take a breath today unless God had given it to me. And He not only gave me that breath, but He gave me His Son as well! And oh, the answer is, 'Yes, I do!!'"

But hast lifted up thyself against the Lord of heaven; and they have brought the vessels of his house before thee, and thou, and thy lords, thy wives, and thy concubines, have drunk wine in them; and thou hast praised the gods of silver, and gold, of brass, iron, wood, and stone, which see not, nor hear, nor know: and the God in whose hand thy breath is, and whose are all thy ways, hast thou not glorified: **Daniel 5:23**

"Do you ever wish you had a different job, Shaniqua?"

"I am just fine, Josh. I make a decent living, have time off to go to church, and I get to meet people like you! What more could a lady want?!"

"Have you heard of that 'Amazing Grace' song? I have heard that one on TV before."

"You're funny, Josh. That song is amazing. You don't have to ask. Here it comes!"

Amazing Grace

*Amazing grace! How sweet the sound
That saved a wretch like me!
I once was lost, but now am found;
Was blind, but now I see.*

'Twas grace that taught my heart to fear,
And grace my fears relieved;
How precious did that grace appear
The hour I first believed.

Through many dangers, toils and snares,
I have already come;
'Tis grace hath brought me safe thus far,
And grace will lead me home.

The Lord has promised good to me,
His word my hope secures;
He will my shield and portion be,
As long as life endures.

Yea, when this flesh and heart shall fail,
And mortal life shall cease,
I shall possess, within the veil,
A life of joy and peace.

The earth shall soon dissolve like snow,
The sun refuse to shine;
But God, who called me here below,
Shall be forever mine.

When we've been there ten thousand years,
Bright shining as the sun,
We've no less days to sing God's praise
Than when we'd first begun.[14]

"One thing you may not know, Josh, is that the author of that song, John Newton, was a very famous slave trader. He worked on slave boats and even captained some that sold slaves in other ports. One thing to remember, Josh, is that if God can forgive a man like John Newton, he literally can forgive any of us. If you will give me about ten more minutes, I will be done with your room. And don't forget, Josh, that it's time for you to get right with Jesus."

Josh doesn't realize it yet, but he will be meeting the Son of God in less than five hours.

I *have no plans* to waste this day. Birthday number 50! No time for a nap, so let's go for a walk here in Paradise!

I went down to the concierge desk, and asked the lady about where I should take a walk. She recommended the Waikiki Historic Trail. A friend of mine back on the mainland told me I needed to make sure to take this walk while I was on the Island, so this is the confirmation I needed. Kanoa gave me a brochure about the trail. "What does your name mean?"

"The free one," she said. "Thanks for asking."

Now that is what I want. Freedom! No rules, live like I want to. Golf some days, make money, go surfing, lay on the beach, and have no worries at all! Freedom! That is what I want for the rest of my long life: Freedom!!

The brochure said:

> The Waikiki Historic Trail is a walking tour of Waikiki, that highlights twenty-three historic sites. Plaques mounted on six-foot tall surfboard-shaped markers have been installed at nineteen of the historic sites. The Waikiki Historic Trail begins on the Diamond Head end of Waikiki and it ends on the grounds of the Hilton Hawaiian Village Resort, after a detour through the Ala Moana and Hawaii Convention Center areas of Honolulu.[15]

Yes, this *is* what my friend was talking about. He said that the stops on the trail would have surfboards cemented into the ground with a plaque on them that tell about each stop on the walk. This is going to be fun. I won't be able to hit all of them, but let me get a few of these in before we go to dinner.

Marker 3 on the trail is pretty interesting. I really like this surfboard! This one is for Queen Lydia Liliuokalani and marks one of the homes she lived in. I have always wanted to be a king! Of course, I could never get a queen to marry me, and I probably couldn't get a whole nation to follow after me either! She was the last Queen of Hawaii. There was actually an attempt to put her back into power, but it failed, and she was arrested. I knew Paradise wasn't boring, but a coup attempt is pretty fascinating!

Now this is one that I have wanted to see, Marker number 5, the *Duke Kahanamoku Statue!*

Duke Kahanamoku became a Hawaiian and United States hero when he won three gold medals and two silver medals in the Olympics. He won one gold and one silver medal at the 1912 Olympics in Stockholm, two gold medals at the 1920 Olympics in Antwerp, and a silver medal at the 1924 Olympics in Paris. Three of his Olympic medals were won in the 100 meter freestyle swimming event, and two were won in the 4x200 meter freestyle relay. Duke Kahanamoku was born on August 24, 1890, and he died of a heart attack on January 22, 1968. In 1984 he was inducted into the United States Olympic Committee Hall of Fame.[16]

This guy was really famous. I remember seeing some things about him on the North Shore this morning, and we ate at his restaurant last night. What an amazing athlete he must have been! He was credited with spreading the sport of surfing to so many different people and places. That sure was a lot of Olympic medals! It reminds me of the flight I took one time when I was sitting across from this Olympic weightlifter. All she talked about was winning a gold medal. So I said to her, "Okay, you win. What are you going to do the next day? And the next?" It seemed like her whole life revolved around getting that medal. I'll never forget that encounter. So Duke, here, won five medals. That's amazing. He got a 9-foot statue out of the deal! I wonder, wherever he is right now, if he's thinking about those five medals?

Marker number 6 doesn't have a surfboard. There is a pile here of sacred stones that are called the ancient healing stones or wizard stones.

> *Regard not them that have familiar spirits, neither seek after wizards, to be defiled by them: I am the LORD your God.*
>
> **Leviticus 19:31**

The way today has been going, I think I am going to pass these wizard stones right on by!

"Hey sir, can you spare me a dollar?"

As I was walking, this homeless man shouted out to me. It is my birthday, so I probably should help the guy.

"It's your lucky day! Yes, I can. What do you need a dollar for?"

"I'm trying to get some *malasadas* from Leonard's Bakery to be honest with you. It's a Portuguese pastry that Hawaii is known for."

"Since it's my birthday, I am going to buy you some *malasadas!*"

"Thank you so much, sir. You just made my day. And just to let you know, it is my birthday, too!!"

"Seriously? What number is it?"

107

"Number 75! What a life!"

"Wow! Today is my 50th. It has been a wonderful day!"

"Your 50th? Very, very interesting. Let's go get those pastries and have a chat."

As we sat down, I said, "My name is Josh. What is your name?"

"It is Keolamauloa. Well, at least that is my Hawaiian name."

"How did you get that name?"

"That is a good question. The name actually means salvation, but there is not a religious reason for why it was given to me. When I first moved over here, a lot of the guys here making these business deals weren't doing such a good job. So many times I had to jump in there and save them! They didn't lose their shirts a few times because of the work that I did, and they were very happy. So they gave me that name. But most people just call me Keo."

"That is interesting. I wish my name meant salvation! It probably would have saved me a lot of heartache. Okay, though, here is my question: If you were doing so good with those business deals, what are you doing living on the streets?"

"Excellent question, Josh. Here comes the answer. I actually moved here with my family on my 50th birthday! It was time for me to come to Paradise, and I did! It was so good at the start. Making big money, working on my golf game, getting a nice tan, etc., but all it took was a few bad business deals, and the money dried up pretty quickly. Funny how everything looked good on the outside with the nice house and the nice car, but it was all a facade. It was amazing how quickly all that wealth disappeared. But when it disappeared, so did my wife. She took the kids and went back to the mainland. I guess I was a little too stubborn. I am a man, and I am going to make it work. Pride is an amazing thing, Josh. You need to watch out for it."

Pride goeth before destruction, and an haughty spirit before a fall. **Proverbs 16:18**

108

"I guess you never thought you would be spending your 75th birthday on the streets."

"No, I didn't, Josh. It has been a good learning experience for me. Now, don't get me wrong, I would much rather live in one of those big houses, but life is so much simpler on the streets. One of the good things about being on the streets here in Hawaii is that you get to see a beautiful sunset and sunrise every day. It sure beats being homeless in a place like Chicago or something."

"I hear you on that one! Can I get a picture with you, Keo?"

"Of course. Just don't sell it and make a lot of money!"

"Let's get that 5-O officer to take it since their station is right there. I don't want to forget this encounter, or this birthday!"

"Never forget, Josh, this isn't Paradise. You won't find it here. Keep searching because it is out there somewhere."

As I head off down the road, why do I get the feeling Keo just gave me a nugget of truth that I will never forget?

Another thing that hits me as I am walking around here is, that there are a lot of homeless people. It just isn't Keo; it's like a lot of homeless people. This is a pretty expensive place to live, but I guess if you are living on the streets, you might as well be in Paradise and homeless, like Keo said, rather than homeless on the streets of New York or Boston. I wonder how they all got here though. Did they hop on a boat and come over? Were they already living here and couldn't pay the bills? This is something that I just didn't expect to see. I don't know if I could ever live on the streets and not have a roof over my head. I like the creature comforts of life too much.

And Jesus saith unto him, The foxes have holes, and the birds of the air have nests; but the Son of man hath not where to lay his head. **Matthew 8:20**

Marker number 11 looks interesting: *Apuakehau Stream and Waikiki Beachboys.*

> The Apuakehau Stream was a favored spot for impromptu evening concerts by the early Waikiki Beachboys.
>
> The largest of Waikiki's three main streams emptied into the sea near where you stand today. The Apuakehau ("basket of dew") flowed through the middle of Waikiki between the ancient areas known as Ulukou and Helumoa until the 1920s. Its waters, which flowed down from Manoa and Palolo Valleys, were then diverted into the Ala Wai Canal.
>
> Apuakehau had always been a favorite spot for the *ali'i*, who enjoyed its cool, clear waters after swimming in the ocean. The mouth of the stream carved out a channel in the ocean bottom that is said to have been the ancient surfing area called Kalehuawehe.[17]

Now, I didn't get too excited because I found out these aren't the real Beach Boys we are talking about here! They were like ambassadors for Waikiki. They could teach people water sports, but many were also musicians. They would play their music, and it kind of lent itself to the romantic side of Waikiki beach.

Again, I am just stunned by the enchanting beauty of this part of the world. It truly seems like Paradise, but maybe not the Paradise that I am looking for.

> *He cutteth out rivers among the rocks; and his eye seeth every precious thing.*   Job 28:10

> *For thus saith the LORD that created the heavens; God himself that formed the earth and made it; he hath established it, he created it not in vain, he formed it to be inhabited: I am the LORD; and there is none else.*   Isaiah 45:18

Marker 14 has piqued my interest: *Afong Villa and Hawaii Army Museum*. I'm almost captivated with it from the start!

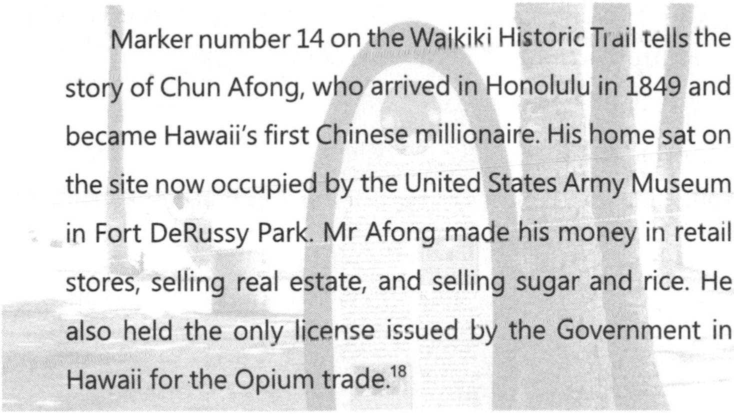

Marker number 14 on the Waikiki Historic Trail tells the story of Chun Afong, who arrived in Honolulu in 1849 and became Hawaii's first Chinese millionaire. His home sat on the site now occupied by the United States Army Museum in Fort DeRussy Park. Mr Afong made his money in retail stores, selling real estate, and selling sugar and rice. He also held the only license issued by the Government in Hawaii for the Opium trade.[18]

Wow, another millionaire! Reminds me of all those mansions that I saw earlier this morning! I can't believe he traded in opium! He would go to jail now!! I have always wanted to be one of those millionaires or billionaires like some of my buddies, or would it be very fleeting just like it was for Keo? Knowing me, it would probably cause me more trouble than any real benefit I would gain from it. But, I am beginning to wonder. All of that money and what did it get him?

> *For what is a man profited, if he shall gain the whole world, and lose his own soul? or what shall a man give in exchange for his soul?* **Matthew 16:26**

Now Marker 16 seems a little familiar to me: *Duke Kahanamoku and the Paoa Estate.* I believe Duke was on one of the previous markers. This guy must have been pretty popular. They obviously have a lot of love and affection for him. He sure did a lot during his life, but I bet it went by quickly. I can't even believe how fast 50 years have gone by for me! At the end of his life, he gets a statue and two markers. I wonder what I am going to have at the end of mine?

> *Whereas ye know not what shall be on the morrow. For what is your life? It is even a vapour, that appeareth for a little time, and then vanisheth away.* **James 4:14**

Marker 21 is the *King David Kalakaua Statue.* They sure like statues around here! Whoever the statue maker guy is, I am sure he got rich!

> Kalakaua moved into his palace with his wife, Queen Kapiolani, the granddaughter of King Kaumualii of Kauai. He decided he needed a more luxurious home, however, and had Iolani Palace built at a cost of $350,000—an unheard of sum at the time.
>
> The Hawaiian culture enjoyed a revival of sorts under Kalakaua, including hula and chants. In July 1887, however, an organization called the Hawaiian League forcibly took control of the government and presented the king with a new constitution. Called the "Bayonet Constitution" (for obvious reasons), Kalakaua had little choice but to sign it. The new constitution severely restricted his powers and signaled the end of the monarchy.
>
> In November 1890, an ill Kalakaua sailed to California for medical treatment. He died at a hotel in San Francisco on January 20, 1891. His final words were, "Tell my people I tried."[19]

He sure sounds like he would have been a fun guy to meet! A little bit of good, a little bit of bad. Kind of like all of us! But, that is it? That is how someone ends their life? Please, "Tell my people I tried"? So when I am on my deathbed, decades from now, I am supposed to look at my wife and kids and say, "I tried my best"?

⌛ *Josh won't be getting a deathbed and decades to live. He will be entering eternity in four short hours.*

4.

I am so glad that I rushed back to the hotel, and am all changed and ready for dinner with all my chums. These are my buddies. My partners in crime back in the day! You don't get a ton of close friends in this lifetime but these guys have been that for me. I am one lucky man to have friends like these!

As we met in the lobby, Michael went up to Kanoa, the concierge, and asked for directions to Hoku's at the Kahala Resort.

"I know you guys are going to thank me later for this, but since it's Josh's birthday, I decided to pick a very special place for us to eat. Hoku's is very famous in these parts, and even better than that, I'm paying! So let's hop in the car and go," Michael said.

Michael has always been such a nice guy. I really liked him all the way back when we first met. That sounds just like him to pick up dinner for my birthday.

When we arrived, the place looked a little too formal for me! I'm more of a regular kind of guy most of the time, but this is nice! I could get used to this. I like it even better when others are paying for it!

As Haloa was walking us to our table, I asked him, "What does your name mean?"

He told me, "Long life."

So I gave him a high five! Not sure that is Hawaiian though! Then he gave me the *shaka* sign, which is when they shake the thumb and the pinky, and it means "cool" or "all is good." Glad my kids found that out and told me before I came over here! Man, I still haven't heard from those kids or my wife all day. Let me send them a quick text. That is me right there: Long life! It's been great to this point, and I can't wait to see how the following years are going to play out!

When our waitress came over, her name tag read, "Paradise"! Why does this not surprise me?! So you know me, here I go again: "Why did your parents name you *Paradise*?"

"Are you sure you want to know?" she responded.

I could already tell there was going to be a story here! "Yes, I do."

"The thing you will see here on the Islands is that people come here because they think this is Paradise. My parents gave me the name but wouldn't tell me why for years. I kept asking, but they wouldn't say. So finally, one day a few years ago in my teens, my parents pulled me aside. They began to tell me why they named me *Paradise*. They told me as I grew up in this world that there would be a lot of lies. A lot of facades. Something might look very good to my eyes, but could either be very evil for me or really just take me down a wrong road."

Love not the world, neither the things that are in the world. If any man love the world, the love of the Father is not in him. For all that is in the world, the lust of the flesh, and the lust of the eyes, and the pride of life, is not of the Father, but is of the world. And the world passeth away, and the lust thereof: but he that doeth the will of God abideth for ever. **1 John 2:15-17**

"They told me to be very careful that my eyes weren't leading me, but something else."

(For we walk by faith, not by sight:) **2 Corinthians 5:7**

"They also told me that so many people will come here to Hawaii to find Paradise, and they won't find it. The brochures are nice, the websites will make this place look wonderful, but a hotel is a hotel, a pool is a pool, a beach is a beach, and a restaurant is a restaurant. And it is a very expensive place to live! So they told me to always remember that our *ohana*—which means 'family' in Hawaiian—friends, and relationships will always be a thousand times more important than searching for Paradise.

114

Utopia is really those folks who are around you right now."

Wow! What an answer! She is so young and yet so deep. "It was worth the trip to Paradise to find out what you, Paradise, had to say about Paradise!"

"Not the answer you were expecting, was it?"

"Not at all. That is why I liked it!"

"Take a look outside. Every table in this restaurant has a panoramic view of the Pacific Ocean. This place is amazing. But really, it is not Paradise. Let me take your drink orders, and I will be back with your menus."

"Boy, did she have a good point! What a good life lesson to learn. I do appreciate your guys' friendship a lot, but I appreciate it much more here in sunny Hawaii than in cold, windy Chicago!"

"We all have so much to be thankful for," Daniel said.

"So here it is my birthday, we just had a wonderful speech from Paradise, and I haven't even gotten a phone call or text from my wife or kids on my 50th birthday!"

"The day is far from over, Josh. Don't give up yet," Michael said.

(Hmmm, almost sounds like he knows something I don't know. But I sure wish I would have heard from them by now.)

Here is what it said on the menu when Paradise brought it to us:

With a twist on contemporary Island cuisine, Hoku's returns to the basics and revamps the classics. The menu has been expanded to include an exotic variety of new dishes, such as Pan Seared Halibut (Avocado Crust, Kamuela Tomato and Maui Onion Salad, Pomegranate Reduction), Maine Lobster Tempura (Sautéed Vegetables, Chili Mint Sauce) and Salt-Crusted Colorado Rack of Lamb Carved Table-Side (Baby Zucchini, Sunburst Squash, Rosemary Jus). The cuisine is fresh, light, and innovative. The ever-popular Hoku's Ahi Musubi and the crisped whole Island Fish (for two) remain on the menu as local favorites. Ingredients are a mix of fresh, locally grown produce and imports from abroad.[20]

I have never let my friends know this, but I have always wanted to be a Sumo wrestler! Now they can tell I am a pretty skinny guy, but this has been one of my dreams. Not because I want to throw salt at another guy and bump bellies with him, but because I love to eat! I mean, just think about that: eat, eat, eat and then bump bellies! That would not be a bad job to have! Well, I didn't attain that in my first fifty years of life, but maybe I will achieve this goal and be a Sumo wrestler in my next fifty years! And tonight, I am going into training!!

When Paradise came back to the table, I asked her, "Do you have any *Loco Moco*?"

She laughed. "Do you know what that is? That is usually a bowl of white rice with a hamburger patty on top and covered with a fried egg and brown gravy. Or as we say, this is Hawaii's version of comfort food! We are way too upscale for that!"

"Okay, how about *Spam Musubi*?"

"You guys are killing me! If you don't know, that is like Spam sushi. We are actually famous for Spam in Hawaii. You can get a Spam cookbook at the store if you want to. Believe it or not, you can actually find it on the breakfast menu at McDonald's! Now, I could ask the chef if he could make you guys either of those two things, but I think he would throw me out of the kitchen! So we better stick to what is on the menu."

So we pretty much ordered one of everything that sounded good and some appetizers. When the appetizers arrived—and boy did the food smell great!—something very, very strange happened.

Michael said, "Hey, guys, why don't we pray before we eat. I will go ahead and do it." And without leaving time for a response, he began, "Father, I just want to thank you so much for this wonderful creation that you have made. It is absolutely amazing to be here. Thank you so much for this grand meal we are about to partake of. Thank you for my three friends here, and please take care of our families back home. Thank you for giving

Josh 50 years of life, and please bless him today on his birthday. And I thank you so much for what your Son Jesus Christ did for me on the cross. I am so humbled and so thankful. And we ask it in His name. Amen."

Then the three of us just kind of raised our heads slowly and looked at Michael in total disbelief. There was that awkward silence at the table. I think all of us, and probably Michael, too, realized that things would be very different from this point forward.

Daniel asked, "What happened to you?!"

"Something did happen to me today, fellas, that has changed my life forever," Michael responded.

"No, Michael. Please don't tell me that you have become one of those 'born-againers,' have you? No, don't tell me that," Daniel replied.

> *Jesus answered and said unto him, Verily, verily, I say unto thee, Except a man be born again, he cannot see the kingdom of God.*   John 3:3

"Let me tell you what happened today, and then we can go from there."

"Are you telling me that the fun-loving, carefree Dr. Michael is long gone? He doesn't exist anymore?" Daniel said.

"Let me tell you what happened, and then give me any feedback that you want to."

Alex and I decided to start digging into the appetizers. We probably didn't want to hear all of this on an empty stomach! But I had a feeling way down deep in me, that something very, very profound had happened to Michael.

"I couldn't sleep this afternoon. Just kind of tossing and turning. So I decided to go for a walk on this stunning day. As I was walking, I ran into a group of guys who were handing out literature, kind of like up at the North Shore today. One of those guys, Jose, started chatting with me. I told him I had a few questions.

"He said, 'Fire away.'

"That was something that really hit me. He had no fear of any question that I asked him. He just answered each one in a very friendly, kind way. He knew his stuff. I like people like that who take the time to search things out just like I try to do. When I had questions about the Bible, he pulled one out and started showing me the answers I was looking for. I then asked him, 'Do you have a seminary degree?'

"He chuckled, 'No, I don't. The Scriptures are pretty simple. God had to make it simple, Michael. Do you know why?'

"I answered, 'No, I don't.'

"So he explained to me, 'In the Bible, God compares us to sheep. He does that numerous times. Now if you know anything about sheep, this may not be the biggest compliment of all time. Sheep can sometimes be some of the dumbest creatures on planet earth! I was watching a video of these sheep, and the first sheep went over a cliff. It was a big cliff, like four hundred feet or so. And as I watched this video on *YouTube*, guess what happened? All of the sheep kept following the first sheep. One by one, they just kept going over the cliff! It was a stunning video. Now a lot of the sheep didn't die. They fell on top of other sheep that had gone over, and they survived, but this video had me mesmerized. Why didn't one of those sheep say, "Hey, don't follow me. I am going over the cliff!"'

"Jose went on to say, 'So I did a little research on sheep. Boy, did I find out some interesting things. Sheep can be very slow to learn and yet demanding at the same time. Sheep can be very stubborn and strong. A sheep might look docile, but if it is running at you, get out of the way because it will hit you like a tank! They are also known to be restless and unpredictable. They are also very well-known to stray. They will wander off and leave the flock. They must be brought back into the fold. Even though they are prone to wander, they are known to be very dependent. They really need the shepherd to be doing the guiding.'"

And Jesus, when he came out, saw much people, and was moved with compassion toward them, because they were as sheep not having a shepherd: and he began to teach them many things. **Mark 6:34**

"Then he made an interesting point. 'So even though a sheep is one of the most amazing creatures that God has ever made, it has some fascinating characteristics. But then I did something one day, Michael, that changed me forever. I looked in the mirror. I began to examine myself. I began to see that all of those same qualities that sheep have were no different than the man that I see every day in the mirror has. This stubborn, foolish man was wandering so far from God, and I knew it was time for a change. And that change happened the day I got saved. I truly needed a Shepherd.'"

For God sent not his Son into the world to condemn the world; but that the world through him might be saved. **John 3:17**

But I receive not testimony from man: but these things I say, that ye might be saved. **John 5:34**

And it shall come to pass, that whosoever shall call on the name of the Lord shall be saved. **Acts 2:21**

"Turning in his Bible, he said, 'Michael, let me show you something from the Scriptures that I literally found life changing.'"

Verily, verily, I say unto you, He that entereth not by the door into the sheepfold, but climbeth up some other way, the same is a thief and a robber. But he that entereth in by the door is the shepherd of the sheep. To him the porter openeth; and the sheep hear his voice: and he calleth his own sheep by name, and leadeth them out. And when he putteth forth his own sheep, he goeth before them, and the sheep follow him: for they know his voice. And a stranger will they not follow, but will flee from him: for they know not the voice of strangers. This parable spake Jesus unto them: but they understood not what things they were which he spake unto them. Then said Jesus unto them again, Verily, verily, I say unto you, I am the door of the sheep. All that ever came before me are thieves and robbers: but the sheep did not hear them. I am the door: by me if any man enter in, he shall be saved, and shall go in and out, and find pasture. The thief cometh not, but for to steal, and to kill, and to destroy: I am come that they might have life, and that they might have it more abundantly. I am the good shepherd: the good shepherd giveth his life for the sheep. But he that is an hireling, and not the shepherd, whose own the sheep are not, seeth the wolf coming, and leaveth the sheep, and fleeth: and the wolf catcheth them, and scattereth the sheep. The hireling fleeth, because he is an hireling, and careth not for the sheep. I am the good shepherd, and know my sheep, and am known of mine. As the Father knoweth me, even so know I the Father: and I lay down my life for the sheep. And other sheep I have, which are not of this fold: them also I must bring, and they shall hear my voice; and there shall be one fold, and one shepherd. Therefore doth my Father love me, because I lay down my life, that I might take it again. **John 10:1-17**

"'Those are the words of Jesus Himself, Michael. It couldn't be said any more perfect than that. He is the Good Shepherd, and I was the wandering sheep. Something had to give here. Either I could keep wandering, or I needed to come back to the Good Shepherd. I have made my decision, Michael. So the real question is, which one will you make?'"

(...behold, now is the accepted time; behold, now is the day of salvation.) **2 Corinthians 6:2**

"So I told Jose, 'I have wrestled with this long enough. It is time to make that decision. What must I do to be saved?'

"He said, 'You sound just like the keeper of the prison in the book of Acts, Michael. Let me show you something.'"

And at midnight Paul and Silas prayed, and sang praises unto God: and the prisoners heard them. And suddenly there was a great earthquake, so that the foundations of the prison were shaken: and immediately all the doors were opened, and every one's bands were loosed. And the keeper of the prison awaking out of his sleep, and seeing the prison doors open, he drew out his sword, and would have killed himself, supposing that the

*prisoners had been fled. But Paul cried with a loud voice, saying,
Do thyself no harm: for we are all here. Then he called for a
light, and sprang in, and came trembling, and fell down before
Paul and Silas, And brought them out, and said, Sirs, what must
I do to be saved? And they said, Believe on the Lord Jesus Christ,
and thou shalt be saved, and thy house.* **Acts 16:25-31**

"Then Jose cautioned me, 'Now, that doesn't mean your whole household will be saved, Michael. Paul knew that when the jailer got saved, it was going to lead to the salvation of his entire family. I have to warn you about something, Michael. This isn't a game. This is serious business. If you want to commit to Jesus and then think it is some get-out-of-hell-free card where you can just do whatever you want after that, you don't have the least understanding of who God is. He hates sin and wants me to hate it, too. There will still be temptations along the way in life. That is what Satan does. Just like when you make a commitment to do something here on earth, it costs you something. Same thing here. When you commit to Jesus, it also costs you something. And that little something is your life!'"

*For whosoever will save his life shall lose it; but whosoever shall
lose his life for my sake and the gospel's, the same shall save it.*
Mark 8:35

"'There is nothing like when you repent of your sins and believe upon the Lord Jesus Christ for the forgiveness of your sins,' Jose explained. 'It is the best decision I've ever made in my life. But one more thing, Michael. Don't think coming to Jesus is going to make life all perfect and sweet and make it this wonderful panacea. I have to be honest, it might even get worse for you.'"

*Yea, and all that will live godly in Christ Jesus shall suffer per-
secution.* **2 Timothy 3:12**

"'Persecution comes with the territory. Even today we are having people mock us because we are out here trying to tell people about sin, repentance, salvation, heaven and hell, and the Judgment to come. Some are interested, and some are not. But I can't worry about that. I know it is my job to seek the lost, just like Jesus did, and share the gospel with them.'"

For the Son of man is come to seek and to save that which was lost.
Luke 19:10

"One thing I liked about Jose was that he was upfront and honest. I wish I had met more people like him during my years of being alive. Yes, today was the day of salvation for me, and I was ready to repent and believe."

Daniel piped in, "So, are you really going to tell us that you now believe Jesus is the only way to heaven? You deal with so many patients from so many backgrounds. Are you telling me you are going to look at that patient who doesn't believe like you do and think that person will rot in the bowels of hell for all of eternity?"

"One thing I've always had to deal with in my life is something called *truth*. If something is true, Daniel, then that means something is false as well. That is just one of those truths of life."

"So, my good friend Michael is now going to be one of those narrow-minded bigots who is going to tell me that there is only one way to get to heaven?"

"What does two plus two equal, Daniel?"

"Four, of course."

"I cannot even begin to believe that you are going to sit here and tell me that there is only one right answer to that question. You are a narrow-minded bigot. Why can't five be the right answer? 55? The reason is, because they are not the right answer. They are wrong. One right answer and an infinite number of wrong answers. What state are we sitting in right now? We are in Hawaii. Not New York, Alabama, or California. One right answer and forty-nine wrong answers. All truth by definition is narrow. So I would also begin to expect eternal truth to be narrow as well."

Daniel said, "That is actually a good point, Michael. I may not agree with your conclusion, but your logic is solid."

"That is the thing. We are all going to die. We are all going to be entering eternity sometime in the near future. All of us here are in our late forties or early fifties. Just think about how quickly life has passed by. It has scooted so quickly. So, even if I live to be one hundred years old, the next fifty will go by just as quickly as the first fifty."

Well, Alex and I are kind of glad that the main courses have just arrived! Paradise is kind of looking at us like, 'what is going on?'! It was funny. I am thoroughly enjoying this conversation. A little tension, but not too much. I am excited to see where this is going to go.

As Daniel dug into his Island Fish, he continued, "All right, Michael, give me your best evidence that there is a God?"

"As you guys enjoy this amazing food, just look outside for me. Look at this creation: sandy beaches, turquoise blue water, the crashing of the waves, all of these exotic flowers, jungles, volcanoes, and even green mountains! You saw all that lush green today as we were driving to the North Shore. Look at the design of all this. Look at how gorgeous and stunning it is. It is so grand and magnificent. The splendor is off the charts with an array of colors, the sweet smells, the island sounds, the balmy breezes, and the late-day sun reflecting off the water. Do you really think this creation happened by luck and by chance over time?"

For the invisible things of him from the creation of the world are clearly seen, being understood by the things that are made, even his eternal power and Godhead; so that they are without excuse: **Romans 1:20**

"Let me give you guys something to look at. Check your phones again."

1. The earth is positioned at just the right distance from the sun so that we receive exactly the proper amount of heat to support life. The other planets of our solar system are either too close to the sun (too hot) or else too far (too cold) to sustain life.

2. Any appreciable change in the rate of rotation of the earth would make life impossible. For example, if the earth were to rotate at 1/10th its present rate, all plant life would either be burned to a crisp during the day or frozen at night.

3. Temperature variations are kept within reasonable limits due to the nearly circular orbit of the earth around the sun.

4. The moon revolves around the earth at a distance of about 240,000 miles, causing harmless tides on the earth. If the moon were located 1/5th of this distance away, the continents would be completely submerged twice a day!

5. The thickness of the earth's crust and the depth of the oceans appear to be carefully designed. Increases in thickness or depth of only a few feet would so drastically alter the absorption of free oxygen and carbon dioxide that plant and animal life could not exist.

6. The earth's axis is tilted 23 degrees from the perpendicular to the plane of its orbit. This tilting, combined with the earth's revolution around the sun, causes our seasons, which are absolutely essential for the raising of food supplies.

7. The earth's atmosphere (especially the ozone layer) serves as a protective shield from lethal solar ultraviolet radiation, which would otherwise destroy all life.

8. The earth's atmosphere also serves to protect the earth by burning up approximately twenty million meteors each day that enter it at speeds of about 30 miles per second! Without this crucial protection, the danger to life would be immense.

9. The two primary constituents of the earth's atmosphere are nitrogen (78 percent) and oxygen (21 percent). This delicate and critical ratio is essential to all life forms.

10. The earth's magnetic field provides important protection from harmful cosmic radiation.[21]

"And since we are here in Paradise, let's learn a little bit more about the air and water that is all around us. Check out the second part of that file."

THE ATMOSPHERE

Ours has been called the "water planet"; it is also the "air planet." These are two special qualities about our world that are not to be found on any of the other planets in our solar system.

The air surrounding our world is called the atmosphere. Air has no color, smell, or taste, yet without it there could be no living plants or animals on the earth. People are known to have survived more than a month without food and more than a week without water. But without air they die within a few minutes.

Without air, there would be no weather. We could have no wind and no storms, which bring us much-needed water. Without wind there would be no movement of the trees and plants and our world would be very still. It would also be silent, for without air we could hear almost nothing. Most sound travels through the air (although some travels through rock, metal, and water). Sound cannot travel in a vacuum.

Without air, birds could not fly. Air provides resistance to motion, and it is this resistance which enables birds and planes to fly through the air. Without air, there would be no clouds. The sky would maintain a dreary blankness day after day. The sky would not be blue; instead, it would be black.

Air is composed of several invisible gases. About 98 percent of those gases are nitrogen and oxygen. Two-tenths of all the air is composed of oxygen (21 percent). Without oxygen we could not survive, for we need it continually in our blood and tissues. Plants would quickly die without it, also. They need it just as they need carbon dioxide.

But eight-tenths of the air is seemingly useless to us; it is nitrogen (78 percent). Surely, it must have a purpose, also; everything else does. Actually, it is invaluable. Oxygen is combustible; that is, it can be set on fire and burn. If there were no nitrogen in the atmosphere, the world would have burned up as soon as the first fire had been ignited by lightning, or the first two flinty rocks striking one another had sparked. Even iron would have burned. We have cause to be very thankful for the nitrogen in the air around us.

The remaining 1 percent of air consists almost entirely of the gas argon. But there are also small amounts of neon, helium, krypton, xenon, hydrogen, ozone, carbon dioxide, nitrous oxide, and methane gases.

All those various gases are invisible. What if they were even slightly opaque? Our world would be totally dark. The gloom of eternal night would be upon us, even though the sun shined brightly overhead. Ocean water looks fairly clear, but 200 feet [61 m] down, the sunlight is nearly gone, and 300 feet [91 m] down, darkness prevails. The atmosphere over our heads is hundreds of miles deep and covers all the earth. If the gases in it were not transparent, we would all live in perpetual darkness. The world would be ice cold. The warming rays of the sun would be blocked out before reaching us. The tiny photosynthesis factories contained within each plant leaf could not operate. No food would be produced, and all the plants and animals would die.

There is also dust in the air. This provides us with beautiful sunset colors on the clouds and in the sky. A cubic inch of air normally has about 100,000 solid particles. The air over the mid-Pacific has about 15,000, and the air above large cities has 5 million particles per square inch.

There are other things in the air also: salt from the ocean, pollen from plants, floating microbes, and ash from meteors which burned upon hitting our atmosphere. There is also water vapor in the atmosphere, and that vapor is vitally important; without it, we would quickly perish! It is part of the water cycle.

Because air has weight, we have barometric pressure, wind movement, and air resistance. The weight of all the air in the world is about 5 quadrillion tons (That is a 5 with 15 zeros after it). The weight of the air in a pint [.47 l] jar is about that of a small capsule or an aspirin tablet. The greatest air pressure is found at the earth's surface, where it averages about 15 pounds [6.8 kg] pressing down on every square inch [2.54 sq cm]. The amount of air pressing down on your shoulders is about 1 ton (1 short ton is 2,000 lbs [907 kg]). Fortunately, you do not feel this weight because it is pressing on you from all sides.

WATER

Another marvelous substance is water which, when pure, is also colorless, odorless, and tasteless. There is a lot of rock and other material beneath our feet, but covering the surface of the planet, there is more water than anything else. Seventy percent of earth's surface is water. Without it, nothing could live. Your body is about two-thirds water.

There are a million million gallons of water in a cubic mile of ocean (that is 1 with 12 zeros after it). Of the 326 million cubic miles [524,631,800 ckm] of water on earth, much of it (97 percent) is in the oceans, but there are also large amounts beneath our feet. The upper half-mile [.8 km] of the earth's crust contains about 3,000 times as much water as all the rivers of earth. Only about 3 percent of the earth's water is fresh. About three-fourths of that fresh water is frozen in glaciers and icecaps. There is as much frozen water as flows in all the rivers in 1,000 years.

We can be thankful that so much water is frozen! If it were to melt, all the seaports of the world would be below the ocean's surface, and much of the continental coastal areas would be lost to us also.

All living things contain lots of water. It is truly the element of life. Your body is about 65 percent water, the same as a mouse. An elephant and an ear of corn are about 70 percent; a chicken is 75 percent water; a potato, earthworm, and pineapple are 80 percent; a tomato is 95 percent; a watermelon about 97 percent.

You can live a month without food, but only a week without water. A person that loses more than 20 percent of his normal water content becomes over-dehydrated and dies a painful death. Each of us must take in about 2 1/2 quarts [2.4 l] of water each day in water and food. On the average, a person takes in about 16,000 gallons [605 hl] of water during his lifetime.

Plants, animals, and people must have a daily inflow of nutrients. Water dissolves those nutrients so they can be carried throughout the body in the blood stream, taken through cell walls, and utilized by the body. The chemical reactions can only take place in a fluid environment. We are here briefly describing processes which are so utterly complex that mankind still has only the barest understanding of them.

Water is needed to grow plants. It requires 115 gallons [435 l] of water to grow enough wheat to bake a loaf of bread. To produce 1 pound [3.7853 l] of potatoes takes 500 pounds [1,892.6 l] of water. About 41 percent of all water used in the United States is for irrigation.

A larger amount, 52 percent, is used to keep the factories going. Without water much of the manufacturing would stop. It takes 65,000 gallons [2,460 hl] to make a ton [.9072 mt] of steel; 10 gallons [37.85 l] to refine a gallon [3.753 l] of gasoline; 250 tons [226.8 mt] to produce a ton [.9072 mt] of paper. In industry, it is especially used to clean, liquidize, but, most of all, to cool.

Without water mankind could accomplish little, much less survive long. Yet it is all based on the water cycle. Water evaporates from oceans, lakes, and rivers. Taken up into the air, it falls as fairly pure water in the form of rain or snow. About 85 percent of the water vapor in the air comes from the oceans. Plants also add moisture to the air. After water is drawn up from the ground through the roots, it passes up to the leaves where it exits as vapor. A typical tree gives off about 70 gallons [265 l] of water a day, and an acre [.4047 ha] of corn gives off about 4,000 gallons [151 hl] a day. This continual drawing of water from the roots up through the stems, trunk, and through the leaves gives turgor (stiffness) to the plants. Without it, they would wilt, become flabby and die.

The oxygen and water given off by plants is part of the reason why you feel more refreshed near plants than in a desert or on a city street.

Water can be a solid, a liquid, or a gas. No other substance appears in these three forms within the earth's normal range of temperature.

Nearly every substance in the world expands as it warms and contracts as it cools. But water is different: As it cools, it continues to contract, and then, a few degrees before it freezes at 32°F [0°C], it begins expanding. As it continues to cool, it continues to expand. For this reason, ice is lighter in weight than an equal amount of water. So the ice floats on water, instead of sinking into it and filling all the lakes and rivers with solid ice in the winter. Because ice expands, the ice sheet on the surface of a pond pushes sideways and locks against the banks on either side. Below it, the water continues to remain liquid, and the ice insulates the water from becoming too cold and freezing also. If it were not for this cooling expansion factor, no plants, fish, frogs, or any other wildlife could survive a winter in rivers and lakes where freezing occurs.[22]

"Now think about that for a second, fellas. It is almost like Someone has finely tuned this universe and with perfect precision set the earth in the exact spot it needs to be from the sun in order to sustain life, and then the atmosphere and the water are balanced perfectly to maintain that life. How could that happen by luck and by chance over time?" Michael reasoned.

"That is a good point," Daniel responded. "There are those days when our family has taken vacations all across the world, and you just look up at the wonder of this universe. You see the stars and the constellations, and you feel so small in all of its vastness that you just begin to wonder."

When I consider thy heavens, the work of thy fingers, the moon and the stars, which thou hast ordained; **Psalm 8:3**

Daniel continued, "Check your phones. Two can play this game!"

"I do not feel obliged to believe that same God who endowed us with sense, reason, and intellect had intended for us to forgo their use."[23]
—Galileo

"The atheist can't find God for the same reason that a thief can't find a policeman."[24]
—Author Unknown

"If there is no God, then all that exists is time and chance acting on matter. If this is true then the difference between your thoughts and mine correspond to the difference between shaking up a bottle of Mountain Dew and a bottle of Dr. Pepper. You simply fizz atheistically and I fizz theistically. This means that you do not hold to atheism because it is true, but rather because of a series of chemical reactions . . . Morality, tragedy, and sorrow are equally evanescent. They are all empty sensations created by the chemical reactions of the brain, in turn created by too much pizza the night before. If there is no God, then all abstractions

are chemical epiphenomena, like swamp gas over fetid water. This means that we have no reason for assigning truth and falsity to the chemical fizz we call reasoning, or right and wrong to the irrational reaction we call morality. If no God, mankind is a set of bi-pedal carbon units of mostly water. And nothing else."[25]
    —Douglas Wilson

"Man is certainly crazy. He could not make a mite, and he makes gods by the dozen."[26]
    —Michel De Montaigne, Essays

"When it comes to God's existence, I'm not an atheist and I'm not an agnostic. I'm an acrostic. The whole thing puzzles me."[27]
    —George Carlin

"If only God would give me some clear sign! Like making a large deposit in my name in a Swiss bank."[28]
    —Woody Allen

"Is man one of God's blunders or is God one of man's blunders?"[29]
    —Friedrich Nietzsche

"Passover is my idea of a perfect holiday. Dear God, when you're handing out plagues of darkness, locusts, hail, boils, flies, lice, frogs, and cattle murrain, and turning the Nile to blood, and smiting firstborn, give me a pass, and tell me when it's over."[30]
    —P.J. O'Rourke, Peace Kills

"How much reverence can you have for a Supreme Being who finds it necessary to include such phenomena as phlegm and tooth decay in His divine system of creation?"[31]
    —Joseph Heller, Catch 22

"I worried about playing God (in the movie Oh God). We're about the same age, but we grew up in different neighborhoods."[32]
    —George Burns, Dr. Burn's Prescription for Happiness

"You are a comedian, Daniel!" I said.

"It was a boring day at work, and we just put some quotes together," he responded.

"Well, one thing is for sure, Daniel," I said trying to get him to think, "Nietzsche, Burns, and Carlin are now 100% assured if there is a God or not. When they died, they either met Him or didn't meet Him. Kind of sobering to think about because it is probably not a joke."

Michael decided to weigh in. "You know, it *is* very sobering to think about. We can all make statements about God, either serious or funny; but we are all going to die, and we are all heading to the other side. It sure makes you want to think about what is over there before you get there."

One thing I have noticed is that Michael is so humble as he has shared all of this with us. It is almost like he is a totally different person.

Therefore if any man be in Christ, he is a new creature: old things are passed away; behold, all things are become new.

2 Corinthians 5:17

"Do you guys remember that philosophy class we all took at Notre Dame? Man, that was a tough class, but I do remember something very specific from it," Alex said. Then he continued, "It was something the professor taught about the Law of Cause and Effect: that every effect had a causation. Your parents caused you, your grandparents caused your parents, etc. So if you keep going back—cause and effect, cause and effect, cause and effect—you eventually have to reach a first cause or an uncaused cause. So there had to be a kick start, so to speak, that kicked the first domino over and caused all the other dominoes to fall over."

"I do remember that very well," I recalled. "I thought that was a great, great point that he made."

"Do you remember the theology class we took?" Alex asked. "I will never forget what I told my mom about that class. I told her that the teacher was an atheist! She was incensed. She couldn't believe that Notre Dame would hire an atheist theology teacher. I mean we are talking about the study of God here!! I remember doing some research for one of the papers I wrote for that class. And what I came up with was creation, design, art, and order. That every creation had a creator, that every design had a designer, that every piece of art had an artist, and every time that we saw order there was an orderer behind it all. So, when you look at this nice table that our food is sitting on, someone created it. Look at Daniel's Rolex. Someone had to design that. Look at that artwork over there on the wall. Someone had to have painted those beautiful paintings. Look at that empty table over there. Look at how all of the knives, forks, and spoons are ordered. Someone had to arrange those. So when we look around the universe, what do we see? We see creation, design, art, and order. If every other thing has a creator, designer, artist, and orderer behind it, why would we not think there is a Creator, Designer, Artist, and Orderer behind this whole universe?"

I responded, "I remember reading that paper you did, now that you mention it, Alex. I actually thought it was a very, very compelling argument that you made. It was so logical. It made my wheels spin when I read it, and I have actually thought about that more than once since then."

Daniel piped in, "Come on, guys. That is nice, but I think it is weak. You can't extrapolate from what you see in an earthly sense to make you think there is a God."

I have always liked making Daniel think, so here I go again! "Daniel, if we took your Rolex and took it apart piece by piece and put it into a shoebox and shook it up, would it shake up into a functioning watch?"

"Of course not."

"Okay, let's say we shook it up for one year. Would it then shake up into a functioning watch?"

"Of course not, Josh."

"Let's say we did that for one million years. Would it shake up into a functioning watch then?"

"Actually more time doesn't help in this example, Josh. It actually makes it less likely over that time frame."

"That is my point, Daniel. Michael laid out some pretty compelling arguments for there being a God, and then Alex followed with some good logic. It would sure seem to me that if your Rolex isn't going to assemble by luck and by chance over time, then neither is this idyllic setting we are sitting in right now, nor those stars or universe we will look up in the sky and see tonight." I continued, "And don't forget all of those fulfilled prophecies that Michael shared with us earlier. This all seems pretty compelling to me."

"Okay then, where did matter come from?" Daniel came back with.

Michael stepped in. "Ahh . . . the age-old question and a good one at that! That is one of the questions I posed to evolutionists through the years. I could never get a solid answer. All they would ever give me is materialism. That matter has always been here, and then we evolved from the matter that was already here. I never really bought that. The reason is, because it takes something to make something. You can't get something from nothing. They were trying to tell me that there was nothing, then a Big Bang happened, and out of that bang we got all of this order and a wonderful creation. I couldn't believe some of my doctor friends would accept something like that. I would ask them, 'Who did the banging? Why did it bang? Since it was nothing, what banged against each other? Why did it bang into something that had order? Every time I see an explosion, like a grenade or gas leak that leads to a house exploding, it sure looks like a whole lot less order happens than more order.' I thought it was a poor argument coming from some very logical people. The only conclusion I could come to is that a Creator would have had to make the first piece of matter, and then that Creator must have made this creation that we live in right now. And I actually think I have found that answer in the Bible. Genesis 1:1 says, '*In the beginning God created the heaven and the earth.*'"

"Oops. Here we go again. You bringing the Bible into this conversation!" Daniel replied.

"Now, Daniel, aren't you Jewish?" Michael said.

"Of course, I am. You know that, Michael."

"So, are you going to tell me that you don't believe in the Torah? You don't believe in the first five books of the Bible? The books of Moses? Are you serious?"

"You want an answer, Michael? You got one. No, I do not. I grew up in a more reformed Jewish household. Kind of the liberal side of Judaism. Again, as I said earlier, it is just more traditions for me and my wife than belief. We do allow the kids to have bar mitzvahs and bah mitzvahs, but after that, we don't force it on them. We are just going to let them make their own choices. Seems like the best thing we can do for them."

I spoke up, "Is your wife Jewish?"

"No, Jannah is actually Muslim."

"What?! Are you serious? How is that working out for you?"

"We have been happily married for many years now. Not too much of an issue. Probably more from her side than my side. I have never told you this before, but when she grew up her family was Hamas. As you probably know, it is a fundamentalist Islamic group in Palestine. Many people look at it as a terrorist group. My wife has completely denounced it, and her family has basically disowned her because of that and because she married a Jewish guy. Have you guys ever seen those COEXIST bumper stickers?

The ones that are blue and white? They usually have the crescent moon of Islam for the 'C,' the Star of David for the 'X,' and the cross of Jesus for the 'T.' You guys have seen those, right?"

"I have actually seen a lot of them during my years," Michael replied.

"Well, that is really what Jannah and I believe. Why can't we all just coexist and get along. Why don't we just let people believe what they want to believe and quit pushing religious beliefs on others. Pretty much just 'live and let live'!"

"So what does your wife think happens when she dies?" I wondered.

"Good question, Josh. She actually still believes in her Islamic faith, which I am totally fine with. She told me that she believes in Paradise and Hellfire when someone dies."

"And what determines who goes where?"

"She said that there is a final judgment in front of Allah where he will judge good and bad deeds. Kind of like the weighing scales that you see in a grocery store. If it weighs towards the good, you get Paradise, and if it weighs towards the bad, you get Hellfire."

"Now, are you going to tell me your wife's name means 'paradise'?"

"Actually, it does!!"

"Why does that not surprise me?! Okay, now back to Paradise for a Muslim. I was chatting with a Muslim man one day, and he told me that when he got to heaven he would have 72 virgins and all of the wine he wanted for eternity. So I asked him how many wives was he allowed to have as a Muslim today? He said that the Qur'an says they can have up to four wives. I asked him if drunkenness was wrong in Islam. He told me that it was. I said, 'Then why would Allah reward you with things that are called *sin* here on planet earth in a place called *Paradise* when we die?' He just looked at me dumbfounded. It just didn't make any sense to me or him once we fleshed it out some."

"I have never thought of it that way before, Josh."

"Also, I remember reading an article about Muhammad Ali one time. He said in the article that every time he signed an autograph, it was one more thing that added up on the good side of the scales which would help him get into Paradise one day."

"Now, hold up," Alex chimed in. "Do you really think there is a God out there that could care less if we signed our names to pieces of paper? That doesn't make a lick of sense to me."

For by grace are ye saved through faith; and that not of your-selves: it is the gift of God: Not of works, lest any man should boast.
Ephesians 2:8,9

"Now, you know that God is going to judge us on our good versus bad works, Alex. That would be the only fair thing He could do," Daniel said.

"I thought you didn't believe in God?" Michael popped in and said.

Daniel laughed. "Even though I don't really believe in one, if there is one, I will be okay because my good works will outweigh my bad ones. I give a lot to charity, I helped plenty of people in NYC after 9/11, I am taking care of my parents, and I continually win yard-of-the-month in my neighborhood! So I should be fine, no matter what."

Michael decided to step in again at this point. "I am going to highly recommend you read the Torah, Daniel. Since the Star of David is on your favorite bumper sticker, you might want to study a little bit more about what they believe."

"What do they believe that I don't know about?"

Michael continued, "You do celebrate the High Holidays, don't you?"

"Yes, my whole family celebrates them, including my wife, by the way."

"So tell me what the Day of Atonement, or Yom Kippur, is all about since it is one of the highest of all the Holy Days to Jews?"

"It *is* the highest of all of the Holy Days for Jews. It has always stood for atonement and repentance. In history, they would take an animal and sacrifice it for the sins of the people. So it represented a new beginning and the cleansing of sins."

> For on that day shall the priest make an atonement for you, to cleanse you, that ye may be clean from all your sins before the LORD.
> **Leviticus 16:30**

Michael answered, "What you had to offer on that day was a perfect blood sacrifice. The lamb could not have any blemish. If you didn't bring a perfect one, the sacrifice wasn't good enough for God."

"Now wait a minute, Michael. We don't have a temple in Jerusalem anymore. There will be a third temple one day, and maybe even soon, but since there is no temple we can't bring God this perfect blood sacrifice you are talking about. Hold up, Michael. No, you are not. Are you going to tell me that Jesus is that perfect blood sacrifice for our sins?"

"So, you have heard that before, Daniel?"

"Yes, some of the Messianic Jews that I have met told me about Jesus being that sacrifice, but they didn't explain it how you just did from the Torah."

> Who needeth not daily, as those high priests, to offer up sacrifice, first for his own sins, and then for the people's: for this he did once, when he offered up himself.
> **Hebrews 7:27**

> For then must he often have suffered since the foundation of the world: but now once in the end of the world hath he appeared to put away sin by the sacrifice of himself. And as it is appointed unto men once to die, but after this the judgment: So Christ was once offered to bear the sins of many; and unto them that look for him shall he appear the second time without sin unto salvation.
> **Hebrews 9:26-28**

"That was the 'aha' moment I had when talking with Jose this afternoon. Finally, two plus two equaled four for me in my quest for spiritual knowledge. Jesus is the long-awaited Messiah and the perfect sacrifice for the sins of the world. *Yeshua Ha Maschiach* as a Jew would say, which means 'Jesus the Messiah.' It all became so crystal clear to me this afternoon."

"Well, this Jew is never going to say that! So, are you now going to tell me that Jesus is the only way to get to heaven?"

"Here you go. Read this. Check your phone!"

John 14:6 "Jesus saith unto him, I am the way, the truth, and the life: no man cometh unto the Father, but by me."

Acts 4:12 "Neither is there salvation in any other: for there is none other name under heaven given among men, whereby we must be saved."

Matthew 7:13,14 "Enter ye in at the strait gate: for wide is the gate, and broad is the way, that leadeth to destruction, and many there be which go in thereat: Because strait is the gate, and narrow is the way, which leadeth unto life, and few there be that find it."

Isaiah 35:8 "And an highway shall be there, and a way, and it shall be called The way of holiness; the unclean shall not pass over it; but it shall be for those: the wayfaring men, though fools, shall not err therein."

1 Timothy 2:4,5 "Who will have all men to be saved, and to come unto the knowledge of the truth. For there is one God, and one mediator between God and men, the man Christ Jesus;"

Romans 3:25 "Whom God hath set forth to be a propitiation through faith in his blood, to declare his righteousness for the remission of sins that are past, through the forbearance of God;"

> Revelation 1:5 "And from Jesus Christ, who is the faithful witness, and the first begotten of the dead, and the prince of the kings of the earth. Unto him that loved us, and washed us from our sins in his own blood,"
>
> John 3:16 "For God so loved the world, that he gave his only begotten Son, that whosoever believeth in him should not perish, but have everlasting life."

"Those sure are a lot of verses, Michael. It seems like God is trying to make it so clear that we can't miss it," I said. "And since you gave some compelling arguments about the proofs for the Bible being true, this is really beginning to make me think."

"Trust me on this, guys. I have had a ton of questions myself. I've had this list of verses in this file for a long, long time while doing my research. When I chatted with Jose today, he began to explain it in such a simple way. He walked me through those verses. He let me know that my works would not be good enough on Judgment Day. God will only accept a blood sacrifice for our sins that is perfect. And Jesus is that one."

For the life of the flesh is in the blood: and I have given it to you upon the altar to make an atonement for your souls: for it is the blood that maketh an atonement for the soul. **Leviticus 17:11**

"So as you can see now, I have no problem saying that Jesus is the only way to heaven because the Bible says it; and Jesus equaled the prophecies, and He rose from the dead, so I can believe what He says. And if He says He is the only way to heaven, and He conquered death to back up that claim, I can believe that and speak it with confidence and authority."

And for me, that utterance may be given unto me, that I may open my mouth boldly, to make known the mystery of the gospel, For which I am an ambassador in bonds: that therein I may speak boldly, as I ought to speak. **Ephesians 6:19,20**

"Well, I am getting the feeling that you are probably going to be my favorite narrow-minded bigot of all time, Michael!" Daniel stated.

Michael replied, "You're funny, Daniel! I have always liked you, and I always will. That will never, ever change for one moment of this lifetime. Don't you ever forget that. But know that I will not just care about you and your family here, but I will also care about where you spend eternity as well."

I can't believe what I just heard. Michael was so, so humble as he said that. He is so caring to each one of us, but especially with Daniel in this back and forth exchange. What a great spirit he has about him. I'm listening to what he has to say, and I can't imagine anyone not listening to him, just by how loving he's coming across.

LORD, thou hast heard the desire of the humble: thou wilt prepare their heart, thou wilt cause thine ear to hear: **Psalm 10:17**

Better it is to be of an humble spirit with the lowly, than to divide the spoil with the proud. **Proverbs 16:19**

Humble yourselves in the sight of the Lord, and he shall lift you up. **James 4:10**

Paradise walked over and said, "Are you *pau*?"

"What does that mean?" I asked.

"It means 'finished.'"

"Finished? You should be in this conversation, Paradise. It is just getting started! But the food is *ono*! Why don't you explain to the guys what that means!"

"That means 'delicious or yummy or the best.' I will tell the chef you said so!"

"Before you go, is that table over there *pau*? That couple by the wall?"

"Yes, they are."

"Please give me their check. I would like to pay for them.

Don't tell them who it is. Just make it a surprise."

"That is one of the nicest things I've ever seen!" Paradise said.

Alex asked, "Why did you do that, Josh?"

"That is the couple I sat next to on the plane flight yesterday when I came in. Boy, do I have a story to tell you about what happened! I don't want to break the flow of this conversation, so I will tell you tomorrow on the links. I have their email, so I will surprise them in a few weeks and tell them who bought their meal."

Daniel stepped in and continued, "That was nice of you, Josh, and those are good points, Michael, but everyone probably needs to check their phone."

1. I already believe in God (Mormonism, Jehovah's Witnesses, Roman Catholic).
2. I'm a good person.
3. All paths lead to heaven.
4. Evolution and geology.
5. The Bible is myth written by men.
6. How can the Christian God judge people who never knew about Jesus.
7. I'm an atheist.
8. Too much evil in the world for there to be a God.
9. My God wouldn't send people to hell.
10. I've been too bad for God to forgive past sins.
11. Hypocrites.

"What is this?" Michael said.

"It is the top ten list for why people won't be an evangelical Christian. We couldn't fit it into ten, so we added an eleventh! You know hedge fund managers can't count very well! The guys and I came up with this list at work one day."

"You guys actually sit around and talk about this?"

"You don't think we just sit around and make millions every day, do you?! You should see the lists that I have on my phone! We need a break at times, and this was one of the good discussions we had!" Daniel said and then added, "It is interesting to watch the atheists in our group. They swear they don't believe in anything, but they sure want to argue that there is no God! It is like they are fighting against something they swear is not there, but deep down really think is there. And it is also interesting to watch them worship the money they make and the materialism that it buys them. It is like they are so duped they can't even see it!"

"You have too much free time on your hands, Daniel! We have dealt with most of those things on your list, so let me just deal with a few others. God doesn't really send people to hell. It is a choice that we get to make to follow Him, or not. So, He will only put His stamp of approval on the choice you make."

I call heaven and earth to record this day against you, that I have set before you life and death, blessing and cursing: therefore choose life, that both thou and thy seed may live: That thou mayest love the LORD thy God, and that thou mayest obey his voice, and that thou mayest cleave unto him: for he is thy life, and the length of thy days: that thou mayest dwell in the land which the LORD sware unto thy fathers, to Abraham, to Isaac, and to Jacob, to give them. **Deuteronomy 30:19,20**

And if it seem evil unto you to serve the LORD, choose you this day whom ye will serve; whether the gods which your fathers served that were on the other side of the flood, or the gods of the Amorites, in whose land ye dwell: but as for me and my house, we will serve the LORD. **Joshua 24:15**

"And another thing to remember, Daniel, is that hell is not a place for people. It was designed for the devil and his angels. People can choose to go there if they reject what Jesus has done for them, but God doesn't take any pleasure in the death of the wicked. He wants them in heaven and not hell. That is why He died for them."

Then shall he say also unto them on the left hand, Depart from me, ye cursed, into everlasting fire, prepared for the devil and his angels: **Matthew 25:41**

Say unto them, As I live, saith the Lord GOD, I have no pleasure in the death of the wicked; but that the wicked turn from his way and live: turn ye, turn ye from your evil ways; for why will ye die, O house of Israel?   **Ezekiel 33:11**

"And one other thing to remember, Daniel, is never worry about hypocrites. Just because we see a few of them while we are down here, doesn't mean there is not a God, or not a heaven and hell. Just think, there are hypocrites in Hawaii. That didn't stop any of us from coming out to vacation here. There are hypocrites in the restaurants that we take our families out to eat in, and they don't stop us from going there. Why would any of us let a hypocrite stop us from finding out about the God who loves us enough to die for every sin that we have ever committed?"

"I am going to have to give that round to Michael! That was a great point!" I said.

"One last question. Let's see if you can score a point on this one to keep Josh happy! The Resurrection. Did Jesus rise from the dead? I really want to know that because I don't think you can believe it or prove it. You are way too logical and rational for that!" Daniel stated.

"If you want a clear, convincing argument, Daniel, I can give you one. Yes, it will be intelligent and plausible. Are you ready?"

"Hit me with it!"

"Here it comes. This will probably be the longest file I have sent you guys today, but trust me, the facts contained therein will be well worth it and more than likely life changing for you."

EVIDENCE FOR THE RESURRECTION
by Josh McDowell

For centuries many of the world's distinguished philosophers have assaulted Christianity as being irrational, superstitious and absurd. Many have chosen simply to ignore the central issue of the resurrection. Others have tried to explain it away through various theories. But the historical evidence just can't be discounted.

A student at the University of Uruguay said to me, "Professor McDowell, why can't you refute Christianity?"

"For a very simple reason," I answered. "I am not able to explain away an event in history—the resurrection of Jesus Christ."

How can we explain the empty tomb? Can it possibly be accounted for by any natural cause?

A QUESTION OF HISTORY

After more than 700 hours of studying this subject, I have come to the conclusion that the resurrection of Jesus Christ is either one of the most wicked, vicious, heartless hoaxes ever foisted on the minds of human beings—or it is the most remarkable fact of history.

Here are some of the facts relevant to the resurrection: Jesus of Nazareth, a Jewish prophet who claimed to be the Christ prophesied in the Jewish Scriptures, was arrested, was judged a political criminal, and was crucified. Three days after His death and burial, some women who went to His tomb found the body gone. In subsequent weeks, His disciples claimed that God had raised Him from the dead and that He appeared to them various times before ascending into heaven.

From that foundation, Christianity spread throughout the Roman Empire and has continued to exert great influence down through the centuries.

LIVING WITNESSES

The New Testament accounts of the resurrection were being circulated within the lifetimes of men and women alive at the time of the resurrection. Those people could certainly have confirmed or denied the accuracy of such accounts.

The writers of the four Gospels either had themselves been witnesses or else were relating the accounts of eyewitnesses of the actual events. In advocating their case for the *gospel*, a word that means "good news," the apostles appealed (even when confronting their most severe opponents) to common knowledge concerning the facts of the resurrection.

F. F. Bruce, Rylands Professor of Biblical Criticism and Exegesis at the University of Manchester, says concerning the value of the New Testament records as primary sources: "Had there been any tendency to depart from the facts in any material respect, the possible presence of hostile witnesses in the audience would have served as a further corrective."

IS THE NEW TESTAMENT RELIABLE?

Because the New Testament provides the primary historical source for information on the resurrection, many critics during the 19th century attacked the reliability of these biblical documents.

By the end of the 19th century, however, archaeological discoveries had confirmed the accuracy of the New Testament manuscripts. Discoveries of early papyri bridged the gap between the time of Christ and existing manuscripts from a later date.

Those findings increased scholarly confidence in the reliability of the Bible. William F. Albright, who in his day was the world's foremost biblical archaeologist, said: "We can already say emphatically that there is no longer any solid basis for dating any book of the New Testament after about A.D. 80, two full generations before the date between 130 and 150 given by the more radical New Testament critics of today."

Coinciding with the papyri discoveries, an abundance of other manuscripts came to light (over 24,000 copies of early New Testament manuscripts are known to be in existence today). The historian Luke wrote of "authentic evidence" concerning the resurrection. Sir William Ramsay, who spent 15 years attempting to undermine Luke's credentials as a historian and to refute the reliability of the New Testament, finally concluded: "Luke is a historian of the first rank. . . . This author should be placed along with the very greatest of historians."

"I claim to be an historian. My approach to Classics is historical. And I tell you that the evidence for the life, the death, and the resurrection of Christ is better authenticated than most of the facts of ancient history . . ."

—E. M. Blaiklock, Professor of Classics, Auckland University

BACKGROUND

The New Testament witnesses were fully aware of the background against which the resurrection took place. The body of Jesus, in accordance with Jewish burial custom, was wrapped in a linen cloth. About 100 pounds of aromatic spices, mixed together to form a gummy substance, were applied to the wrappings of cloth about the body. After the body was placed in a solid rock tomb, an extremely large stone was rolled against the entrance of the tomb. Large stones weighing approximately two tons were normally rolled (by means of levers) against a tomb entrance.

A Roman guard, of strictly disciplined fighting men, was stationed to guard the tomb. This guard affixed on the tomb the Roman seal, which was meant to "prevent any attempt at vandalizing the sepulcher." Anyone trying to move the stone from the tomb's entrance would have broken the seal and thus incurred the wrath of Roman law.

But three days later, the tomb was empty. The followers of Jesus said He had risen from the dead. They reported that He appeared to them during a period of 40 days, showing Himself to them by many "infallible proofs." Paul the apostle recounted that Jesus appeared to more than 500 of His followers at one time, the majority of whom were still alive and who could confirm what Paul wrote. So many security precautions were taken with the trial, crucifixion, burial, entombment, sealing, and guarding of Christ's tomb that it becomes very difficult for critics to defend their position that Christ did not rise from the dead. Consider these facts:

FACT #1: BROKEN ROMAN SEAL

As we have said, the first obvious fact was the breaking of the seal that stood for the power and authority of the Roman Empire. The consequences of breaking the seal were extremely severe. The FBI and CIA of the Roman Empire were called into action to find the man or men who were responsible. If they were apprehended, it meant automatic execution by crucifixion upside down. People feared the breaking of the seal. Jesus' disciples displayed signs of cowardice when they hid themselves. Peter, one of these disciples, went out and denied Christ three times.

FACT #2: EMPTY TOMB

As we have already discussed, another obvious fact after the resurrection was the empty tomb. The disciples of Christ did not go off to Athens or Rome to preach that Christ was raised from the dead. Rather, they went right back to the city of Jerusalem, where, if what they were teaching was false, the falsity would be evident. The empty tomb was "too notorious to be denied." Paul Althaus states that the resurrection "could have not been maintained in Jerusalem for a single day, for a single hour, if the emptiness of the tomb had not been established as a fact for all concerned."

Both Jewish and Roman sources and traditions admit an empty tomb. Those resources range from Josephus to a compilation of fifth-century Jewish writings called the "Toledoth Jeshu." Dr. Paul Maier calls this "positive evidence from a hostile source, which is the strongest kind of historical evidence. In essence, this means that if a source admits a fact decidedly not in its favor, then that fact is genuine."

Gamaliel, who was a member of the Jewish high court, the Sanhedrin, put forth the suggestion that the rise of the Christian movement was God's doing; he could not have done that if the tomb were still occupied, or if the Sanhedrin knew the whereabouts of Christ's body.

Paul Maier observes that " . . . if all the evidence is weighed carefully and fairly, it is indeed justifiable, according to the canons of historical research, to conclude that the sepulcher of Joseph of Arimathea, in which Jesus was buried, was actually empty on the morning of the first Easter. And no shred of evidence has yet been discovered in literary sources, epigraphy, or archaeology that would disprove this statement."

FACT #3: LARGE STONE MOVED

On that Sunday morning, the first thing that impressed the people who approached the tomb was the unusual position of the one and a half to two ton stone that had been lodged in front of the doorway. All the Gospel writers mention it.

Those who observed the stone after the resurrection describe its position as having been rolled up a slope away not just from the entrance of the tomb, but from the entire massive sepulcher. It was in such a position that it looked as if it had been picked up and carried away. Now, I ask you, if the disciples had wanted to come in, tiptoe around the sleeping guards, and then roll the stone over and steal Jesus' body, how could they have done that without the guards' awareness?

FACT #4: ROMAN GUARD GOES AWOL

The Roman guards fled. They left their place of responsibility. How can their attrition be explained, when Roman military discipline was so exceptional? Justin, in Digest #49, mentions all of the offenses that required the death penalty. The fear of their superiors' wrath and the possibility of death meant that they paid close attention to the minutest details of their jobs. One way a guard was put to death was by being stripped of his clothes and then burned alive in a fire started with his garments. If it was not apparent which soldier had failed in his duty, then lots were drawn to see which one would be punished with death for the guard unit's failure. Certainly the entire unit would not have fallen asleep with that kind of threat over their heads. Dr. George Currie, a student of Roman military discipline, wrote that fear of punishment "produced flawless attention to duty, especially in the night watches."

FACT #5: GRAVECLOTHES TELL A TALE

In a literal sense, against all statements to the contrary, the tomb was not totally empty—because of an amazing phenomenon. John, a disciple of Jesus, looked over to the place where the body of Jesus had lain, and there were the grave clothes, in the form of the body, slightly caved in and empty—like the empty chrysalis of a caterpillar's cocoon. That's enough to make a believer out of anybody. John never did get over it. The first thing that stuck in the minds of the disciples was not the empty tomb, but rather the empty grave clothes—undisturbed in form and position.

FACT #6: JESUS' APPEARANCES CONFIRMED

Christ appeared alive on several occasions after the cataclysmic events of that first Easter. When studying an event in history, it is important to know whether enough people who were participants or eyewitnesses to the event were alive when the facts about the event were published. To know this is obviously helpful in ascertaining the accuracy of the published report. If the number of eyewitnesses is substantial, the event can be regarded as fairly well-established. For instance, if we all witness a murder, and a later police report turns out to be a fabrication of lies, we as eyewitnesses can refute it.

OVER 500 WITNESSES

Several very important factors are often overlooked when considering Christ's post-resurrection appearances to individuals. The first is the large number of witnesses of Christ after that resurrection morning. One of the earliest records of Christ's appearing after the resurrection is by Paul. The apostle appealed to his audience's knowledge of the fact that Christ had been seen by more than 500 people at one time. Paul reminded them that the majority of those people were still alive and could be questioned. Dr. Edwin M. Yamauchi, associate professor of history at Miami University in Oxford, Ohio, emphasizes: "What gives a special authority to the list (of witnesses) as historical evidence is the reference to most of the five hundred brethren being still alive. St. Paul says in effect, 'If you do not believe me, you can ask them.' Such a statement in an admittedly genuine letter written within thirty years of the event is almost as strong evidence as one could hope to get for something that happened nearly two thousand years ago." Let's take the more than 500 witnesses who saw Jesus alive after His death and burial and place them in a courtroom. Do you realize that if each of those 500 people were to testify for only six minutes, including cross-examination, you would have an amazing 50 hours of firsthand testimony? Add to this the testimony of many other eyewitnesses, and you would well have the largest and most lopsided trial in history.

HOSTILE WITNESSES

Another factor crucial to interpreting Christ's appearances is that He also appeared to those who were hostile or unconvinced.

Over and over again, I have read or heard people comment that Jesus was seen alive after His death and burial only by His friends and followers. Using that argument, they attempt to water down the overwhelming impact of the multiple eyewitness accounts. But that line of reasoning hardly deserves comment. No author or informed individual would regard Saul of Tarsus as being a follower of Christ. The facts show the exact opposite. Saul despised Christ and persecuted Christ's followers. It was a life-shattering experience when Christ appeared to him. Although he was at the time not a disciple, he later became the apostle Paul, one of the greatest witnesses for the truth of the resurrection.

"If the New Testament were a collection of secular writings, their authenticity would generally be regarded as beyond all doubt."

—F. F. Bruce (Manchester University)

The argument that Christ's appearances were only to followers is an argument for the most part from silence, and arguments from silence can be dangerous. It is equally possible that all to whom

Jesus appeared became followers. No one acquainted with the facts can accurately say that Jesus appeared to just "an insignificant few."

Christians believe that Jesus was bodily resurrected in time and space by the supernatural power of God. The difficulties of belief may be great, but the problems inherent in unbelief present even greater difficulties.

The theories advanced to explain the resurrection by "natural causes" are weak; they actually help to build confidence in the truth of the resurrection.

THE WRONG TOMB?

A theory propounded by Kirsopp Lake assumes that the women who reported that the body was missing had mistakenly gone to the wrong tomb. If so, then the disciples who went to check up on the women's statement must have also gone to the wrong tomb. We may be certain, however, that Jewish authorities, who asked for a Roman guard to be stationed at the tomb to prevent Jesus' body from being stolen, would not have been mistaken about the location. Nor would the Roman guards, for they were there!

If the resurrection-claim was merely because of a geographical mistake, the Jewish authorities would have lost no time in producing the body from the proper tomb, thus effectively quenching for all time any rumor of resurrection.

HALLUCINATIONS?

Another attempted explanation claims that the appearances of Jesus after the resurrection were either illusions or hallucinations. Unsupported by the psychological principles governing the appearances of hallucinations, this theory also does not coincide with the historical situation. Again, where was the actual body, and why wasn't it produced?

DID JESUS SWOON?

Another theory, popularized by Venturini several centuries ago, is often quoted today. This is the swoon theory, which says that Jesus didn't die; he merely fainted from exhaustion and loss of blood. Everyone thought Him dead, but later He resuscitated, and the disciples thought it to be a resurrection. Skeptic David Friedrich Strauss—certainly no believer in the resurrection—gave the deathblow to any thought that Jesus revived from a swoon: "It is impossible that a being who had been stolen half-dead out of the sepulchre, who crept about weak and ill, wanting medical treatment, who required bandaging, strengthening and indulgence, and who still at last yielded to His sufferings, could have given to the disciples the impression that He was a Conqueror over death and the grave, the Prince of Life, an impression which lay at the bottom of their future ministry. Such a resuscitation could only have weakened the impression which He had made upon them in life and in death, at the most could only have given it an elegiac voice, but could by no possibility have changed their sorrow into enthusiasm, have elevated their reverence into worship."

"For the New Testament of Acts, the confirmation of historicity is overwhelming. Any attempt to reject its basic historicity, even in matters of detail, must now appear absurd. Roman historians have long taken it for granted."

—A. N. Sherwin-White (Classical Roman Historian)

THE BODY STOLEN?

Then consider the theory that the body was stolen by the disciples while the guards slept. The depression and cowardice of the disciples provide a hard-hitting argument against their suddenly becoming so brave and daring as to face a detachment of soldiers at the tomb and steal the body. They were in no mood to attempt anything like that.

The theory that the Jewish or Roman authorities moved Christ's body is no more reasonable an explanation for the empty tomb than theft by the disciples. If the authorities had the body in their possession or knew where it was, why, when the disciples were preaching the resurrection in Jerusalem, didn't they explain: "Wait! We moved the body, see, He didn't rise from the grave"?

And if such a rebuttal failed, why didn't they explain exactly where Jesus' body lay? If this failed, why didn't they recover the corpse, put it on a cart, and wheel it through the center of Jerusalem? Such an action would have destroyed Christianity—not in the cradle, but in the womb!

THE RESURRECTION IS A FACT

Professor Thomas Arnold, for 14 years a headmaster of Rugby, author of the famous, *History of Rome,* and appointed to the chair of modern history at Oxford, was well-acquainted with the value of evidence in determining historical facts. This great scholar said: "I have been used for many years to study the histories of other times, and to examine and weigh the evidence of those who have written about them, and I know of no one fact in the history of mankind which is proved by better and fuller evidence of every sort, to the understanding of a fair inquirer, than the great sign which God hath given us that Christ died and rose again from the dead." Brooke Foss Westcott, an English scholar, said: "taking all the evidence together, it is not too much to say that there is no historic incident better or more variously supported than the resurrection of Christ. Nothing but the antecedent assumption that it must be false could have suggested the idea of deficiency in the proof of it."

REAL PROOF: THE DISCIPLES' LIVES

But the most telling testimony of all must be the lives of those early Christians. We must ask ourselves: What caused them to go everywhere telling the message of the risen Christ?

Had there been any visible benefits accrued to them from their efforts—prestige, wealth, increased social status or material benefits—we might logically attempt to account for their actions, for their whole-hearted and total allegiance to this "risen Christ."

As a reward for their efforts, however, those early Christians were beaten, stoned to death, thrown to the lions, tortured and crucified. Every conceivable method was used to stop them from talking.

Yet, they laid down their lives as the ultimate proof of their complete confidence in the truth of their message.[33]

"I have to tell you something, Michael. I am not easily persuaded." Daniel explained, "I have a very analytical mind, and that has helped me to become very, very successful in the hedge fund world. That is some extremely compelling evidence. I have had others try to explain that to me, but never to this level or depth of knowledge. I want to thank you that because that powerful evidence has me thinking."

"One last thing for you guys to look at."

Dr. Greenleaf, the Royal Professor of Law at Harvard University, was one of the greatest legal minds that ever lived. He wrote the famous legal volume entitled, *A Treatise on the Law of Evidence,* considered by many the greatest legal volume ever written. Dr. Simon Greenleaf believed the Resurrection of Jesus Christ was a hoax. And he determined, once and for all, to expose the "myth" of the Resurrection. After thoroughly examining the evidence for the resurrection—Dr. Greenleaf came to the exact opposite conclusion! He wrote a book entitled, *An Examination of the Testimony of the Four Evangelists by the Rules of Evidence Administered in the Courts of Justice,* in which he emphatically stated:

> *"It was IMPOSSIBLE that the apostles could have persisted in affirming the truths they had narrated, had not JESUS CHRIST ACTUALLY RISEN FROM THE DEAD..."*[34]

Greenleaf concluded that according to the jurisdiction of legal evidence the resurrection of Jesus Christ was the best supported event in all of history![35]

"Not only was Dr. Greenleaf convinced of the resurrection of Jesus Christ, Daniel, he committed his life to Jesus Christ just as I have done today! I can deny this truth no longer. But remember, if Jesus didn't rise from the dead, then this is all one big joke. It is Donald Duck and Mickey Mouse. It is a fairytale and nothing less than that. Literally, someone's faith would be in vain if the tomb was not empty."

And if Christ be not raised, your faith is vain; ye are yet in your sins.   **1 Corinthians 15:17**

"Do you remember the account I told you of the student at Clemson who had the evil, hissing laughter experience when her soul exited her body? She asked me what she must do to never experience that again. I didn't have an answer for her then. I do have an answer for her now, and that is Jesus. That is the same answer that I want to give you, some of my best friends that I have ever had, as well. I have been so thankful for your friendships through the years, but I want to make sure we are eternal friends as well."

Daniel smirked and said, "Well, I'm glad that you have an answer for her, Michael. But I live by the Golden Rule: He who has the most gold, makes the rules! That is what I'm striving for."

Alex spoke up, "You know, if this is our last supper together, it was a great one! But I am beginning to think that we spent all this time to plan a week's vacation, and I have not spent enough time planning for eternity."

"Okay, let's make a pact, Michael," Daniel said and then continued, "We have heard you on this, and thanks for taking the time to share what you have shared. But let's make a pact that you will never bring this up again. I want to make sure that we will be able to continue our friendships in the days to come."

"No, I cannot make a commitment that I cannot keep, Daniel. I hear what you are saying, but I plan on continuing our friendship and continuing to share eternal truth with you until I take my last breath or until you take your last breath."

Why do I get the feeling this is going to be a dinner that I will never forget?

"One more thing, Josh. This is for you!"

Michael handed me this carved, wooden plaque. "What is this?"

"Hawaii is well-known for its koa wood. And one of the best gifts you can get for someone is something made from this wood. So this is a mini koa surfboard plaque with a laser-engraved surf scene from the North Shore. We hope it will always remind you of your 50th birthday and remind you of Paradise!"

These guys are too much. What more can a man ask from his friends!

"Thank you so much. This is an impressive piece of artwork. It will look great in my home. Thank you." I admired my gift for a moment but then realized the sun was dropping lower in the sky. I said, "Now this has been fun, guys, but let's hustle back to the hotel because I want to see the sunset tonight."

"That is a good idea," said Michael. "For all we know, there might be something special waiting for us back at the hotel!"

I am beginning to wonder if he knows something and is just not telling me.

"I want to see a bunch of those sunsets here in Paradise this week!"

Little does Josh know, but this will be the final sunset he will ever see. He will be dead in three hours.

3.

On the car ride back, I did want to pose a question to Michael. "You have done a lot of research, Michael, and I always appreciate how you search things out. You will go in-depth until you find your answer. A simple question for you: What about evolution?"

"That is one of the big questions we must all wrestle with at some point in our lives. We know what we have been taught, but the real question is, what is true? All of us had evolution taught to us in our schools, and we had it taught to us at Notre Dame. I was teaching a class one time to some medical students, and a couple of young men came up to me after the class and challenged me with something. Now, you guys know I like to think, so I never mind that at all. They said, 'Have you ever studied the truth claims about Creationism?' I was kind of blown away when they asked that. I didn't even know there were truth claims about Creationism! So, I asked them to give me some information.

"Here we go again: Check your phones!!"

> According to Dr. Kent Hovind, the test of any theory is whether or not it provides answers to basic questions.
>
> **How Would You Answer These?**
>
> 1. When, where, why, and how did life come from non-living matter?
>
> 2. When, where, why, and how did life learn to reproduce itself?
>
> 3. With what did the first cell capable of sexual reproduction reproduce?

4. Why would any plant or animal want to reproduce more of its kind since this would only make more mouths to feed and decrease the chances of survival? (Does the individual have a drive to survive, or the species? How do you explain this?)

5. How can mutations (recombining of the genetic code) create any new, improved varieties? (Recombining English letters will never produce Chinese books.)

6. Natural selection works only with the genetic information available and tends only to keep a species stable. How would you explain the increasing complexity in the genetic code that must have occurred if evolution were true?

7. When, where, why, and how did:
    a) Single-celled plants become multi-celled? (Where are the two- and three-celled intermediates?)
    b) Fish change to amphibians?
    c) Amphibians change to reptiles?
    d) Reptiles change to birds? (Their lungs, bones, eyes, reproductive organs, heart, method of locomotion, body covering, etc., are all very different!) How did the intermediate forms live?

8. When, where, why, how, and from what did:
    a) Whales evolve?
    b) Sea horses evolve?
    c) Bats evolve?
    d) Hair, skin, feathers, scales, nails, claws, etc., evolve?

9. Which of the following evolved first (how, and how long, did it work without the others)?
    a) The digestive system, the food to be digested, the appetite, the ability to find and eat the food, the digestive juices, or the body's resistance to its own digestive juice (stomach, intestines, etc.)?
    b) The drive to reproduce or the ability to reproduce?
    c) The lungs, the mucus lining to protect them, the throat, or the perfect mixture of gases to be breathed into the lungs?
    d) The plants, or the insects that live on and pollinate the plants?
    e) The bones, ligaments, tendons, blood supply, or muscles to move the bones?
    f) The immune system or the need for it?[36]

"As you guys know, I am a thinker. I just love it! These young men presented me with some questions that got my wheels spinning. And after hours and hours of research, I could not say that evolution answered those questions. I was literally stunned. I had even been teaching this to students, even though I had never really taken the time to process it myself. I couldn't believe how foolish I was. Now look at the last part of the file and look at these quotes."

> "All those trees of life with their branches of our ancestors, that's a lot of nonsense."[37]
> —Mary Leakey
>
> "The evolutionary trees that adorn our textbooks have data only at the tips and nodes of their branches; the rest is inference, however reasonable, not the evidence of fossils."[38]
> —Dr. Stephen Jay Gould, Harvard University
>
> "The absence of fossil evidence for intermediary stages has been a persistent and nagging problem for evolution."[39]
> —Dr. Stephen J. Gould, Harvard University
>
> "In the years after Darwin, his advocates hoped to find predictable progressions. In general, these have not been found—yet the optimism has died hard, and some pure fantasy has crept into the textbooks."[40]
> —David M. Raup

Luther Sunderland asked evolutionists what evidence they had for their theory. The British Museum of Natural History has the largest fossil collection in the world. When the senior paleontologist (Colin Paterson) was asked why he did not show the missing links in his book, he said:

> "I fully agree with your comments on the lack of evolutionary transitions in my book. If I knew of any, fossil or living, I would certainly have included them. I will lay it on the line—there is not one such fossil."[41]
> —Dr. Colin Paterson, Senior Paleontologist, British Museum of Natural History

"The universe and the laws of physics seem to have been specifically designed for us. If any one of about 40 physical qualities had more than slightly different values, life as we know it could not exist: Either atoms would not be stable, or they wouldn't combine into molecules, or the stars wouldn't form the heavier elements, or the universe would collapse before life could develop, and so on..."[42]

–Stephen Hawking, Austin American Statesman

"Researchers suggest that virtually all modern men—99% of them, says one scientist—are closely related genetically and share genes with one male ancestor, dubbed 'Y-chromosome Adam.' We are finding that humans have very, very shallow genetic roots which go back very recently to one ancestor... That indicates that there was an origin in a specific location on the globe, and then it spread out from there."[43]

–US News and World Report

"Darwin admitted that millions of 'missing links,' transitional life forms, would have to be discovered in the fossil record to prove the accuracy of his theory that all species had gradually evolved by chance mutation into new species. Unfortunately for his theory, despite hundreds of millions spent on searching for fossils worldwide for more than a century, the scientists have failed to locate a single missing link out of the millions that must exist if their theory of evolution is to be vindicated."[44]

–Grant R. Jeffery, *The Signature of God*

"The likelihood of the formation of life from inanimate matter is one out of 10 to the power of 40,000 . . . It is big enough to bury Darwin and the whole theory of evolution. There was no primeval soup, neither on this planet nor on any other, and if the beginnings of life were not random, they must therefore have been the product of purposeful intelligence."[45]

–Sir Fredrick Hoyle, Professor of Astronomy, Cambridge University

Sir Arthur Keith *(Evolution and Ethics)* wrote:
"The conclusion I have come to is this: the law of Christ is incompatible with the law of evolution, nay, the two laws are at war with each other."[46]

He also wrote:

"Evolution is unproved and improvable. We believe it because the only alternative is special creation, and that is unthinkable."[47]

Professor Louis Bounoure, Director of Research, National Center of Scientific Research stated:

"Evolution is a fairytale for grown-ups. This theory has helped nothing in the progress of science. It is useless."[48]

Malcolm Muggeridge, the famous British journalist and philosopher said:

"I myself am convinced that the theory of evolution, especially the extent to which it's been applied, will be one of the great jokes in history books of the future."[49]

"My personal feeling is that understanding evolution led me to atheism."[50]

–Richard Dawkins

"We are the product of 4.5 billion years of fortuitous, slow biological evolution. There is no reason to think that the evolutionary process has stopped. Man is a transitional animal. He is not the climax of creation."[51]

–Carl Sagan

"I am quite conscious that my speculations run quite beyond the bounds of true science."[52]

–Charles Darwin, *In a letter to Asa Gray, a Harvard Professor of Biology. Quoted in N.C. Gillespie, 'Charles Darwin and the Problem of Creation' (1979), p. 2 [University of Chicago book]*

"To suppose that the eye with all its inimitable contrivances for adjusting the focus to different distances, for admitting different amounts of light, and for the correction of spherical and chromatic aberration, could have been formed by natural selection, seems, I freely confess, absurd in the highest degree."[53]

–Charles Darwin, *(Origin of Species, Ch. 6, p.144)*

"As you can tell, these medical students gave me a lot to chew on. Those are my kind of students! And the conclusion I came to was that all I was doing was repeating and regurgitating what my teachers and professors had taught me for years. I had never taken the time to process it and think it through for myself. I just took it carte blanche. Even these quotes tell you that so many evolutionists had questions themselves that could not—and I mean could not—be answered by science. But I had decided it was true, and I wasn't going to question it. I can't even tell you how disappointed I was in myself when I realized what I had done. But the real problem was what I had not done. I had not taken the time to use my own brain to do my own research. How sad that is for a learned man like myself."

"Don't be too hard on yourself, Michael," I responded. "You have finally come to your own conclusion. You know the answer now."

"Oh, my research wasn't done. It was time for me to look at some of the creations on planet earth. I wanted to look a little deeper at some more evidence. Is it possible that they did evolve, or were there animals and creatures that literally defied evolution?

"One more time! Check your phones!"

DOLPHINS AND WHALES

We can demonstrate one such transition problem by using the example of dolphins and whales. These mammals bear their young alive and breathe air, yet spend their entire lifetime in the sea. Presumably, in order for dolphins and whales to have evolved, they must have originated from a land mammal that returned to the water and changed into a sea creature. But dolphins and whales have so many remarkable features upon which their survival depends that they couldn't have evolved! It would be a lot like trying to change a bus into a submarine, one part at a time, all the while it is traveling at 60 miles per hour.

The following is a list of transitions evolutionists have to account for in the dolphin in its evolution from some unknown land dwelling pre-dolphin:

- The nose would have to move to the back of the head.
- Feet, claws, or tail would be exchanged for fins and flippers.
- It would have to develop a torpedo-shaped body for efficient swimming in the water.
- It would have to be able to drink sea water and desalinize it.
- Its entire bone structure and metabolism would have to be rearranged.
- It would need to develop a sophisticated sonar system to search for food.

Could the dolphin acquire these features gradually one at a time over a period of millions of years? What about the transitional stages? Would they have survived with just some of these features? Why is there a total absence of transitional forms fossilized?

Consider the whale and its enormous size in comparison with the plankton it feeds upon. The whale is a nautical vacuum cleaner, with a baleen filter. While it was "developing" this feature, what did it feed upon before? For me, it takes a great stretch of the imagination to picture the evolution of dolphins and whales.[54]

CREATION WINS BY A NECK

Have you ever wondered why the giraffe's brain doesn't explode when he stoops to get a drink of water? Or, why he doesn't pass out when he raises his head back up again? It's because God has specially created valves in his neck which close off the enormous flow of blood needed to raise it to the giraffe's great height.

The giraffe has a powerful heart almost two feet long to make sure the blood supply gets to his brain. But if he did not have the special valves in his arteries which regulate his blood supply, his brain would explode under the pressure. Also, there is a special sponge underneath the giraffe's brain which absorbs the last pump of blood. Now, when he raises back up, that sponge squeezes that oxygenated blood into his brain, the valves open up, and he doesn't pass out.

Now, could this mechanism have evolved? No way! If the first giraffe had a long neck and two-foot long heart, but no mechanism to regulate it, when he first stooped to get a drink of water, he would have blown his mind. Then, after he had blown his mind, he would have thought to himself, "I need to evolve valves in my arteries to regulate this!" No, he would have been dead! The giraffe's long neck couldn't have evolved; it needed to be completely functional in the first place.[55]

EUROPEAN EEL RETURNS HOME

The Sargasso Sea is an immense patch of water in the tropical Atlantic, which is filled with a variety of seaweed and small creatures. It lies between Bermuda and the West Indies.

Among those who journey there are small eels. Upon arrival, they seem to know exactly what to do. Going to a depth of about

1,300 to 2,500 feet, they lay their eggs and then leave. The parent eels do not see their young and never give them any training. Soon after, the parents die.

In this deep, 20°C cold, the eggs hatch into slender, transparent eels that look different than their parents. Even their fins are located in different places. Because of where the eggs were laid, the young are gradually carried eastward at a depth of 700 feet into the Gulf Stream. Northward it takes them, and on and on they are carried.

Scientists have dropped labeled logs into the ocean where the eggs are laid, and ten months later they arrive off the coast of Europe. The little eels make the same trip, but for some unexplained reason, do it in a year and a half. But these little creatures are not logs! When the wood reaches Europe, it just keeps sailing on past down the coast. But when the eels reach that large continent, they know to go up just certain rivers, into certain tributaries, and thence into certain lakes, the very ones their parents used to live in. Arriving in those lakes, the young will know to depart through certain streams, and finally go back to the same brooks where their parents lived for several years!

But let us return to the time they arrive off the coast of Europe. When they reach the edge of the continental shelf, which may be several hundred miles from land, their bodies begin changing. Until now, they have not needed complicated swimming gear, for they were carried along by the Gulf current. But now, at just the right time, their bodies change. But why are their bodies triggered to do it just then?

Their leaf-shaped body narrows, they shrink a little in length, and grow pectoral fins. Soon they look like their parents, but are a little smaller and still transparent. With this change completed, something inside tells them they must invade Europe. They also know that they have so much work ahead of them for a while, they must stop eating.

Some go into Britain, others into the Baltic, still others up the rivers of France, and others go through the Straits of Gibraltar into the Mediterranean. Some go all the way to the Black Sea. Arriving at their appointed place by the coast, they know that they must now enter fresh water—and keep going. Swimming up the rivers, they remain within a yard of the bank, thus avoiding the rapid current out in the middle. Because they are transparent, they are unnoticed by most predators. Stubbornly persistent, they avoid waterfalls by wriggling through the sodden vegetation on the banks. When they enter lakes, their sensitivity tells them which feeder river to journey up.

After they have been in fresh water several months, they begin eating again. Now they grow to their full adult size and opaque appearance, with yellow backs and sides. They remain in these streams for several years, moving to lower, warmer streams in the winters and higher again in the summers.

Scientists have caught eels in a Scandinavian estuary, tagged and released them in another over a hundred miles away. Within weeks they had returned to their original feeding grounds. Others have been caught and taken several hundred yards away and placed on the ground. They always know which direction to wriggle in order to again return to the stream. This they do even when a rise in the ground obstructs their view and they have to wriggle upward.

After the males have been in the rivers for three years, and the females for eight or nine, they again change—this time from yellow to black.

Very soon they will need to be as dark as possible in order to remain hidden. Their eyes enlarge because, to do what is ahead of them, they will need much sharper vision.

And now, something tells them that the time has come.

Down they go—from stream to lake, and from lake to river; downward, onward—until they reach the sea. When placed in a pond at this time, they will wriggle out of it and cross dew-drenched fields in order to reach rivers that will take them to the ocean. They know they must return to the sea. But there the track was lost; what happened to them then? Recently, scientists embedded tiny radio transmitters beneath their skin. We now know that, arriving at the ocean, they swim away from the European coast in a north-westerly direction at a depth of about 200 feet until they reach the continental shelf. The seafloor then drops to 3,000 feet, and they quickly dive to about 1,400 feet. Then they swim away to the southwest.

A map of the Atlantic Ocean reveals that such a course will take them back to the Sargasso Sea where they were born so many years before. Six months later, their tiny radios show them reappearing in the Sargasso Sea—3,500 miles from their little river streams.

But how did they know where to go? Even if they did know, how could they find their way to that location through oceans—which to them are uncharted. "Uncharted," I say, for people may have charts, but the wildlife does not. How then can they know where to go and how to get there? Regarding the second question, researchers tried a number of experiments and found that the eels may be guided by the stars in their initial ocean travels, as they swim near the surface till they reach the continental shelf. But what is their means of guidance after that? Try diving down to 1,400 feet into the ocean, and then figure out where to go. It is pitch black in those depths, and you could not see a compass even if you had one in your hand. Do they detect very low frequency vibrations from the waves overhead? Yet passing storm fronts bring continual confusion to wave motion on the surface.

So, arriving in the Sargasso Sea, they have now laid their eggs. Their young, when hatched, will never be taught by them the journey they must make, for no adult eel has ever traveled from the Sargasso Sea to Europe, or, arriving there, initially swam up its rivers. It is a trip that only their babies will make.

After so many years absence, the parents have returned to their birthplace. They have spawned, and now they swim away and die. They have come to the end of their journey.[56]

RADAR JAMMING AND STEALTH PLANES

As the little bat flies through the darkness, its sonar squeaks give its brain a picture of what is ahead as it searches for flying insects.

But the moth (apparently, all moths) can hear its high-pitched squeak from 100 feet away. This is an advantage, since the bat can only receive echoes from 20 feet. Intercepting the bat signals, which tell it that the bat is drawing near, the moth knows that it must suddenly go into a free fall. Why does it know that a bat squeak means imminent death? Once a moth is swallowed by a bat, it cannot warn its offspring. Until it is swallowed, it cannot know that danger is there. But now the little moth is falling for its life, and its only hope of safety is to suddenly drop to the ground. But the bat may catch the falling moth in its sonar. Going after the moth, the bat comes closer. But the moth resorts to aerobatics, and flits this way and that. It only has a few feet to go before reaching the protective ground.

Some tiger moth species have a sonar jamming device. This is an ultrasonic sound that throws bats off course. Using some of the techniques employed by the millions-of-dollars stealth plane, the tiger moth makes it to safety as the bat heads off toward where he thought the return echo was coming from.

Can the U.S. military use a cheaper stealth bomber? (It is presently the most expensive plane in the world!) Go to the tiger moth and ask him how he does it. He never paid a dollar for his equipment. He didn't think it up either; it was given to him.[57]

THE NOSE HAS IT

The dog has an amazing sense of smell. This makes up for their poor eyesight. A dachshund, for example, has about 125 million smell-detecting cells in its nose. A human being has only 5 million. A German shepherd dog has 230 million, making its sense of smell more than a million times more sensitive than a human's. A bloodhound has a sense of smell equal to that of the German shepherd. There must be genetic factors in the odors we produce. George Romanes, in 1885, showed that skilled tracker dogs could differentiate between anything, except identical twins. To the dog, the twins smelled exactly the same.

By the way, dogs also have good hearing. They can hear high-pitched sound frequencies of up to 40,000 vibrations a second. A human being cannot go beyond 20,000 vibrations per second.[58]

THE GECKO LIZARD

Next, consider the amazing gecko lizard, which can walk across the ceiling upside down without falling off. On its toe pads are an estimated 500 million tiny fibers tipped with little suction cups. In addition, the tips of the lizard's toes bend upward so that it can peel off the suction cups gradually at each step and not get stuck to the surface.

Dr. Robert Kofahl explains:

"The extraordinary microscopic structure of the gecko lizard's toe pads clearly indicates intelligent purposeful design. No remotely plausible scheme for the origin of the gecko's suction cups by random mutations and natural selection has yet been proposed by evolutionary theorists. And should some scientist with a clever imagination succeed in devising such a scheme, he would still be without a scrap of fossil evidence to demonstrate that the hypothetical process of evolution actually took place in the past."[59]

Why would the process of random mutations and blind chance put suction cups on the gecko's feet? Only half a suction cup would make the gecko lunch for some other creature! Too much suction and the gecko isn't going anywhere!

How did mindless evolution know to also create toes that curl upward to control the suction? Only the hand of God could have created the purposeful design of the gecko lizard.

THE DRAGON FLY

The dragonfly is another amazing icon of creation. There are nearly 5,000 varieties, ranging in size from 3/4 inch to 7 1/2 inches. An extinct variety measured 30 inches from wing tip to wing tip.

Consider its life cycle. It hatches from an egg in a larval form called a nymph that lives in the water and breathes through internal gills. The nymph is ugly and colorless, but it has a "jet propulsion" system whereby it squirts water out rapidly to create fast movement when alarmed. After a few months to three years, the nymph crawls out of the water, begins to breathe air, attaches itself to the stem of a plant, undergoes metamorphosis in one night, and emerges from its larval body as a beautiful, flying, air-breathing dragonfly. Though it has lived in the water all its life until this point, it is immediately an expert flyer and spends most of the rest of its life flitting through the air like an insect edition of the hummingbird.

Consider its eyes. It has two large compound eyes, each composed of up to 30,000 facets containing a lens installed at a perfect angle in conjunction with all of the other lenses. This gives it a nearly 360 degree field of vision. It also has three smaller simple eyes called ocelli on the top and front of its head. 80% of its mental processes are devoted to vision. It sees in color and can detect ultraviolet light. The dragonfly's vision is so amazing that it is being studied by the Australian National University with the goal of improving robot flight. Dr. Richard Berry, who is in charge of this project, says, "The ocelli of dragonflies are exceptionally well-tuned to provide fast, sensitive and directionally selective information about the world."[60]

Consider its wings. The wing membranes are thinner than paper and very strong. They are reinforced by veins or tubes only 1/10th of a millimeter thick, which act as "spars" for the wings as well as tubes for the cables of the nervous system and for the transportation of the blood fluid. Consider its flying ability. It can fly up, down, sideways, or backwards and can change direction in an instant. It can glide. It can hover and then rapidly accelerate up to 35 miles per hour. It can beat each pair of wings together or separately; the rear wings can be out of phase with the front wings; and it can even move each wing independently, thus allowing for extreme maneuvers. It can catch other flying insects, such as flies and mosquitoes, in the air, either with its mouth or by forming a little basket with its legs and their bristly spines.

Its amazing neck muscles allow the dragonfly to move its head sideways 180 degrees, back 70 degrees, and down 40 degrees.

Consider its beauty. Dragonflies are brilliantly colored and typically are multi-colored. They can be green, yellow, blue, red, fuchsia, maroon, orange, pink, gold, and black. The colors come in earth tones as well as metallic varieties. These are formed in three ways: pigmentation (e.g., melanin produces yellows, reds, and browns), wax coating that diffuses light (similar to the coating on some shiny fruits), and light reflecting chitin scales, which perfectly diffract various parts of the light wave to create brilliant metallic colors.[61]

"Just think about the intricacies of these creatures," Michael explained. "Many of these you will see here in Hawaii, but be careful of that dragonfly with the 30-inch wingspan! How did these animals evolve? They couldn't have. Now keep reading. It even gets more exciting!"

CIRCULATORY SYSTEM

If I tried to put an ad in the newspaper announcing houses that come with self-manufacturing plumbing and electrical systems, they would tell me I was writing science fiction and refuse to print it. If I tried to have it printed in a science magazine, they would laugh in my face. But that is what your body does. Before you were born, it constructed its own plumbing and electrical system—and more besides.

Your body is filled with plumbing; in fact, with several totally different plumbing systems. These include your circulatory system, which sends blood all over your body, your urinary system, which purifies the blood, and your lymphatic system, which carries on additional cleaning actions in body tissues. There are also compact plumbing systems in the liver, kidneys, mammary glands, skin, sweat and oil glands, and the endocrine glands.

Your circulatory system is composed of a blood pump (your heart) and the plumbing (blood vessels) needed to carry fluid (blood) throughout your body.

The structure of the heart is another great marvel. It is perfectly designed for what it must do and is the hardest working muscle in your body. In the wall of the right atrium of the heart is a small spot of tissue. Called the sino-atrial (SA) node, approximately every second this tissue sends out a tiny electrical signal which special nerves quickly carry throughout the heart muscle in the right ventricle. The message it sends is: "Beat!" Instantly, a second node, the atrioventricular (AV) node is alerted and relays the message on to the left ventricle: "Beat!"

And your heart beats! Moment by moment, day by day, year by year, it keeps beating. How thankful are you for that beating heart?

The heart is a powerful pump that drives 5 to 6 quarts [4.7-5.7 liters] of blood per minute through several miles of tubes in your body. During active exercise, this can go up to 20 quarts [19 liters]. Consider the complicated, yet efficient design of the pump.

Blood from all parts of your body returns through the superior and inferior vena cava (the largest veins in your body) and enters a "waiting room," the right atrium (right auricle), ready to enter the right ventricle. When the next heart beat occurs, the ventricles squeeze. The load of blood already in the right ventricle is squeezed out into the pulmonary artery (and is sent to the lungs for oxygen). None of that blood flows back into the ventricle, because the semilunar valve guards the exit. That same squeeze brought the waiting blood from the right atrium through the tricuspid valve into the right ventricle. That valve keeps it from flowing back into the right atrium.

Blood returning from the lungs passes through four pulmonary veins into the left atrium (left auricle). A mural (bicuspid) valve guards the entrance into the left ventricle. Then comes the next heartbeat which sends that blood into the left ventricle, a split second after the blood in the ventricle has been squeezed out through the semilunar valve into the aorta (the largest artery in your body).

The blood in the aorta goes to all parts of your body. From the aorta, that crimson stream is carried to still smaller arteries, and thence into arterioles. These flow through capillaries so tiny that the blood cells must pass single file. As they do, oxygen and nutrients pass across into the cells, while carbon dioxide and wastes leave the cells and pass out into the capillaries. Still other waste pass out into the lymph vessels to be carried away. From the capillaries, the blood passes into venules veins, then into then into the inferior or superior vena cava, and back to the heart. Random activity of molecules is supposed to have invented all that? Why, the organism would be long dead before "natural selection" ever got started trying to figure out such complication! Natural selection is simply random activity, and nothing more; it does not have the brains to accomplish anything worthwhile.

Your blood cells are very complex . . . we discuss part of the immense requirements needed to invent blood and other body cells. There are different types of blood cells; each one is vital, and each one contains hundreds of key factors needed for life. Complicated enzymes must be present to produce the crucial ingredients in those cells.

One cubic centimeter—smaller than a drop of blood—contains an average of 4.5-5 million red blood cells. They wear out in less than a month, and more are made in the red bone marrow. That same cubic centimeter of blood contains 7,000-9,000 white blood cells, and increases to 15,000-25,000 when infection occurs. There are several types of white blood cells. That same cubic centimeter of blood contains 250,000-500,000 blood platelets (thrombocytes). If you cut your finger, these are used to quickly clot the blood so you will not bleed to death.

The above description is over-simplified in the extreme. But it is enough to take one's breath away! A powerful and extremely intelligent Being created you!

In addition to the blood circulatory system, there is the lymphatic system. If all your body were removed except your lymph vessels, the complete three-dimensional form of your body would still be there. That is how many lymph vessels there are in your body! Your lymphatics are used to carry away additional wastes from your cells.[62]

"Now check out these amazing facts about the human body!"

1. The stomach's digestive acids are strong enough to dissolve zinc. Fortunately for us, the cells in the stomach lining renew so quickly that the acids don't have time to dissolve it.

2. The lungs contain over 300,000 million capillaries (tiny blood vessels). If they were laid end to end, they would stretch 2400 km (1500 miles).

3. Human bone is as strong as granite in supporting weight. A block of bone the size of a matchbox can support 9 tonnes—that is four times as much as concrete can support.

4. Each finger and toenail takes six months to grow from base to tip.

5. The largest organ in the body is the skin. In an adult man, it covers about 1.9 m^2 (20 sq ft). The skin constantly flakes away—in a lifetime each person sheds around 18 kg (40 lb) of skin.

6. When you sleep, you grow by about 8 mm (0.3 in). The next day you shrink back to your former height. The reason is that your cartilage discs are squeezed like sponges by the force of gravity when you stand or sit.

7. The average person in the West eats 50 tonnes of food and drinks 60,000 liters (16,000 gallons) of liquid during his life.

8. Each kidney contains 1 million individual filters. They filter an average of around 1.3 liters (2.2 pints) of blood per minute, and expel up to 1.4 liters (2.5 pints) a day of urine.

9. The focusing muscles of the eyes move around 100,000 times a day. To give your leg muscles the same workout, you would need to walk 80 km (50 miles) every day.

10. In 30 minutes, the average body gives off enough heat (combined) to bring a half gallon of water to boil.

11. A single human blood cell takes only 60 seconds to make a complete circuit of the body.

12. The eyes receive approximately 90 percent of all our information, making us basically visual creatures.[63]

"After listening to a lecture on evolution by a science professor, a student wrote a poem and titled it 'The Amazing Professor.' The poem read: Once I was a tadpole when I began to begin. Then I was a frog with my tail tucked in. Next I was a monkey on a coconut tree. Now I am a doctor with a Ph.D."[64]

—Anonymous

"Darwin's ominous book [*Origin of Species*] had been available in Bronn's translation for two years. The German professional zoologists, botanists and geologists almost all regarded it [Darwin's theory] as absolute nonsense. Agassiz, Geibel, Keferstein, and so many others, laughed until they were red in the face—"[65]

—Wilhelm Bölsche

"From a tadpole to a Dr. with a Ph.D.! That had me laughing and so sad at the same time. That was me until I wised-up. So as you can see, I found out that 'goo to the zoo to you' was incredibly false! I cut bodies open all the time. I should have known better. You just read all those facts about this amazing body each one of us has. How could two people, a male and a female, evolve at the exact same time, at the exact same place, with completely different reproductive organs that had to be working perfectly for that species to continue? Absolutely impossible! I saw the design of the human body every single day and just denied it. How could I have done that? All this time I thought I was this highly evolved creature, and little did I know I was one of those special one-of-a-kind people, and that was so much better to find out than being a highly evolved ape!"

"So it is just that simple, Michael? God created it all, and we are His creations?" I asked.

"I really believe it is that simple, Josh. Now all we have to do is find out who He is. Yes, that simple."

Daniel spoke up, "What has happened to us, fellas? We used to talk about sports, the Fighting Irish, making millions, our kids, etc. This is getting way too deep. We need to slow down some."

Josh is not slowing down but speeding towards eternity, and he will be there in two hours. Will he choose to simply believe before it is too late, or simply head off into eternity unprepared to meet his Maker?

I am so glad that we got back to the hotel when we did. Time to dress down a little bit and go find a nice bench by the beach and check out this sunset before twilight. I have heard they are gorgeous, and I have seen the pictures, but I know for sure that the real deal will be better than all of those! Pictures can't do justice to the real thing. Tonight is going to be a night I will never forget!

As I walked out of the hotel and onto the sidewalk, and as I caught a gust of the trade winds, I wondered who are those people on the street corner over there? Kind of looks like that Darrel guy I met today. Let me just stand a few feet away and listen. They sure are holding up some interesting signs! Three of the signs they are holding up say, "WHERE WILL YOU SPEND ETERNITY?" "ASK ME WHY YOU DESERVE HELL?" and "THERE IS ROOM AT THE CROSS FOR YOU."

Tonight's dinner and now this? You would almost think this is a sign or something for me! Why would these guys be out here doing this? It almost seems like such a foolish way to spend a beautiful evening, a whole day, or even a lifetime.

For the preaching of the cross is to them that perish foolishness; but unto us which are saved it is the power of God. For it is written, I will destroy the wisdom of the wise, and will bring to nothing the understanding of the prudent. Where is the wise? where is the scribe? where is the disputer of this world? hath not God made foolish the wisdom of this world? For after that in the wisdom of God the world by wisdom knew not God, it pleased God by the foolishness of preaching to save them that believe. For the Jews require a sign, and the Greeks seek after wisdom: But we preach Christ crucified, unto the Jews a stumblingblock, and unto the Greeks foolishness; But unto them which are called, both Jews and Greeks, Christ the power of God, and the wisdom of God. Because the foolishness of God is wiser than men; and the weakness of God is stronger than men. For ye see your calling, brethren, how that not many wise men after the flesh, not many mighty, not many noble, are called: But God hath chosen the foolish things of the world to confound the wise; and God hath chosen the weak things of the world to confound the things which are mighty;   1 Corinthians 1:18-27

The way today has been going, I might as well go up and chat with these guys. I will still have time to make it over to the beach for the sunset.

"Hey, how are you guys doing tonight?" I said as I walked up to them.

"We are doing fine this evening," one of them responded.

"What is that you're handing out?" I realized after I asked that these cards were similar, but different from the ones Darrel was handing out this afternoon. "Why does it say 'What If?' on there?"

"That is what is called a gospel tract. We are asking people like you 'what if' today was your last day on planet earth, where do you think you would spend eternity?"

"Okay. Slow down there, guys. What are your names first?"

"We are Zach, John, David, and Chris. And the guy over there chatting with that person is with us as well."

"My name is Josh. Nice to meet you. Please tell me the main reason you are out here tonight?"

Zach, who was doing the speaking for the group at this time said, "Josh, once you know there is a God and there is a heaven and a hell, and Jesus is the only One that can forgive you of your sins, you want to tell everyone you can about that!"

"Can't you just let people enjoy the sunset this evening?"

"We are trying to tell you, Josh, Who is the One that is about to paint those beautiful colors all across the sky as the sun falls below the horizon."

"You really think there is a God who is going to do that?"

"I know so, Josh."

"So before I walk away and watch the sunset, why do I deserve hell?"

"Good question, Josh. All sinners deserve the wrath of God. He is a holy being Who is without sin. He hates sin. It is repulsive to Him. Your sins are a stench to His nostrils. His wrath is going to fall on you unless you repent of your sins and believe upon the Lord Jesus Christ for the forgiveness of your sins."

> *For the wrath of God is revealed from heaven against all ungodliness and unrighteousness of men, who hold the truth in unrighteousness;* **Romans 1:18**

> *Exalt ye the LORD our God, and worship at his footstool; for he is holy.* **Psalm 99:5**

> *Repent ye therefore, and be converted, that your sins may be blotted out, when the times of refreshing shall come from the presence of the Lord;* **Acts 3:19**

"Okay. Thank you very much. I'll take your gospel tract and look it over later."

"Remember, Josh, as you pass those palm trees, that when you see a tree, your gift isn't under a tree, it is on a tree! He died for your sins, Josh. Please take this seriously."

> *And he is the propitiation for our sins: and not for ours only, but also for the sins of the whole world.* **1 John 2:2**

"I have a Bible in my hotel room. I should probably pick it up tonight and take a gander at it."

"Read and heed." Zach continued, "And don't forget, if Jesus isn't your Master, you are headed for disaster!"

"Thanks, fellas."

185

"Be careful, Josh. Time is a precious commodity. It scoots by very quickly. None of us knows how much time we have left down here."

So teach us to number our days, that we may apply our hearts unto wisdom.   **Psalm 90:12**

"Come on, guys. I am still young. Today is my 50th birthday! I am very excited. There is no need to sing for me! I plan on having many more of these birthdays, and hopefully spending a few of them here in Hawaii!"

For a thousand years in thy sight are but as yesterday when it is past, and as a watch in the night.   **Psalm 90:4**

All of a sudden, that other guy jumped into the conversation. "Hello, my name is Jose. I overheard you say that it is your 50th birthday. Do you know a doctor named Michael?"

I am sure I had a very surprised look on my face before I responded. I wondered if this could possibly be the same 'Jose' who talked with Michael today? My head is spinning. This is getting to be too much for me. I hesitated for a second, but then had to ask, "Are you the 'Jose' who talked with Michael today?"

"You know about that?" Jose responded.

"Please, tell me about the encounter you had with him today."

"He was out walking this afternoon, and he and I had a very fascinating give and take. He said he was out here with some college chums, and they were celebrating one of the guy's 50th birthday. So I kind of put two and two together as I overheard part of your conversation. You do know that he passed from death to life today, don't you?"

Verily, verily, I say unto you, He that heareth my word, and believeth on him that sent me, hath everlasting life, and shall not come into condemnation; but is passed from death unto life.
John 5:24

"What do you mean by that?"

"He got saved today, Josh. He became born again. And when you become born again like the Bible talks about, you can know exactly—and I do mean exactly—where you will go when you die. Michael passed from eternal death in hell to everlasting life with Jesus today!"

And this is the record, that God hath given to us eternal life, and this life is in his Son. He that hath the Son hath life; and he that hath not the Son of God hath not life. These things have I written unto you that believe on the name of the Son of God; that ye may know that ye have eternal life, and that ye may believe on the name of the Son of God. **1 John 5:11-13**

"Let me tell you something, Jose. Believe it or not, Michael shared all of that and a whole lot more at dinner tonight. He is literally a changed man. I could see it in his eyes and countenance. He had such a humble demeanor to him. His voice was strong and authoritative as he spoke to us, but he had so much caring in his voice as well. It was very obvious that he cared about our souls and cared where all of us were going to spend eternity."

Likewise, I say unto you, there is joy in the presence of the angels of God over one sinner that repenteth. **Luke 15:10**

"That is why we are out here, Josh. We care about your soul as well. Please heed what Michael said to you and what we have said to you this evening."

"Thanks for not yelling at me, fellas. Thanks for sharing what you believe. I appreciate it, and it is kind of you. Thanks for caring about me. I can't even say that about some of my co-workers that I have worked with for years, but for some reason, I really do believe you care about me. I'll take the time to think through what you have shared."

Josh is forty-five minutes away from eternity. Time is not on Josh's side, and he still doesn't know it.

As I began to walk away, I realized those guys had given me a lot to think about. I sauntered over to find a bench to sit on with a perfect view of the sand and ocean, and found one. Not too many people around. This is good. I really believe I have a lot to contemplate before the sun begins to set.

What a warm, gorgeous evening. This is literally Paradise! I was right. I knew it all along. Chicago in the winter—no way! I am going to come here every year at this time whether I'm with my friends or not!

"*Aloha ahiahi,*" a man said as he approached the bench.

"What does that mean?" I responded.

"It means good evening."

"Well, you have that right! What a gorgeous evening it is!"

"May I sit down?"

"Sure."

"Is this your first sunset in Hawaii?"

"You could tell?"

"Oh, you have that excited look of anticipation on your face! I have seen it before."

"Well, I am not a rookie to sunsets, but I am definitely a rookie to Hawaiian sunsets!"

"What you are going to see tonight will most likely be different than so many other sunsets you have seen."

That they may know from the rising of the sun, and from the west, that there is none beside me. I am the Lord, and there is none else. **Isaiah 45:6**

Just then, I remembered the brochure that the concierge handed me earlier in the afternoon that described Hawaii's stunning sunsets.

A large part of Hawaii's spiritual draw can be attributed to its unique and inspirational sunset views. Gorgeous red, orange, pink and blue hues leave spectators in awe as the sun makes its way toward the horizon. The ubiquitous sunshine that provided 12 hours of life-giving light and beach and outdoor fun sinks peacefully into the sea as if being tucked in after a hard day's work...

At the time of sunset, more light is piercing the atmosphere than at any other time during the day. The heating process during the day has created a high number of particles in the air, which are able to scatter more light. We know that sunsets derive their red hues because the long wavelengths are the least scattered. The geography of Hawaii, tropical temperatures, humidity levels and a variety of other factors combine to give us the original palette we see as the sun sets.[66]

"And with those low clouds in the sky, you are going to see colors popping off everywhere, and with the clouds moving, the shapes will change as well. This is really going to be a spectacular light show tonight!"

"So, you are a local?"

"Yes."

"And this doesn't get boring to you?"

"This place never gets old. This creation just screams with the fingerprints of God. I look at that sunset and that unbelievable light, and it reminds me of Who put this whole place together. No, it doesn't ever get boring!"

"Hold up now. You are not one of those Bible-thumper guys like I saw on the streets over there, are you?"

"Are you asking me if I believe in God?"

"Okay, let's go there. Yes, I am asking that."

"I really think it takes more faith to believe that this whole universe happened by luck and by chance over time, than it does to believe that God created it. I guess I don't have enough faith to be an atheist!"

"That's funny. People always think atheists have the evidence on their side, but you think the evidence points to a God creating all of this?"

"Look at evidence to determine everything you do in life. I noticed you are not looking in the other direction expecting a sunset. For all we know, the sun might just reverse its course and set in the opposite direction! But you have done this before. You can see all of the other folks out here looking in the same direction, so the evidence tells us that the sun will probably descend in the direction everyone is looking. So evidence is important to look at every time we make a decision."

"Considering how my day has been going, one of my buddies has basically given me a science lesson today on the topic of God and the evidence for His existence! His evidence was compelling. So I won't argue with his logic because the facts he laid out satisfied my inquisitive mind."

"Since you have come to the conclusion that there is God, that would then beg the next question: What do you think happens after we die?"

"Whatever it is, I will be okay. I have been a good guy for most of my life, and I have no plans to stop now!"

Most men will proclaim every one his own goodness: but a faithful man who can find? **Proverbs 20:6**

"Do you think it might be reincarnation?"

"It might just be. I wouldn't mind a few more go rounds at this life! My golf game might improve a few lifetimes from now!"

And as it is appointed unto men once to die, but after this the judgment: **Hebrews 9:27**

 190

"Do you think it could be a heaven or hell when you die?"

"That is probably where I am leaning the most right now."

"The Bible says that is where people go when they die. One or the other."

If I ascend up into heaven, thou art there: if I make my bed in hell, behold, thou art there.   **Psalm 139:8**

"My friend, who gave me the science lesson on God, also gave me a lesson about the Bible being true. Again, his logic and facts were irrefutable to be honest with you. It was very impressive."

"Since your friend gave all of that to you and you seem to be convinced of it, if you would die today, would you go to heaven or hell?"

"Most definitely heaven. My ticket is punched for that place. My goods works definitely outweigh my bad, and they will take me right where I want to go when I die. No worries here."

"Interesting. Have you ever thought about the fact that maybe God will judge by a different standard than being good?"

"No way. Everything in life is predicated on good vs. bad. I get my raises and promotions if I do well. If my employees do a good job, they keep their job. If they don't, they lose that job. I got more playing time in college if I was playing well. Everything in life is that way, so I am sure it is that way when we die."

"That raises an interesting point. Just because we have standards here, those might not be God's standards. And since you have said the arguments for the Bible are compelling and irrefutable, then we can go there for some answers.

"The God of the Bible is the Creator of the universe, and He made man in His image. We are spiritual beings just like He is. God is eternal, and so are we. He is also immutable. That word means 'unchanging.' He is the same yesterday, today, and forever! So in essence, you can count on Him."

For I am the LORD, I change not; therefore ye sons of Jacob are not consumed. **Malachi 3:6**

God is not a man, that he should lie; neither the son of man, that he should repent: hath he said, and shall he not do it? or hath he spoken, and shall he not make it good? **Numbers 23:19**

They shall perish, but thou shalt endure: yea, all of them shall wax old like a garment; as a vesture shalt thou change them, and they shall be changed: But thou art the same, and thy years shall have no end. **Psalm 102:26,27**

Jesus Christ the same yesterday, and to day, and for ever. **Hebrews 13:8**

"God is incomparable. There is no one and nothing like Him. All the descriptions we can muster up can't really do justice to who He is. He can't be dissected even though we try to do that all the time."

Wherefore thou art great, O LORD God: for there is none like thee, neither is there any God beside thee, according to all that we have heard with our ears. **2 Samuel 7:22**

Be ye therefore perfect, even as your Father which is in heaven is perfect. **Matthew 5:48**

"But even though we can't really know who God is, He has given us this irrefutable book called the Bible that does tell us things about Him. It uses words to describe Him, so we can too. He is a just God. He is also all-powerful and all-knowing. He is also present everywhere, but that doesn't mean He is *in* everything. It never says that in the Scriptures."

As for God, his way is perfect: the word of the LORD is tried: he is a buckler to all those that trust in him. **Psalm 18:30**

O LORD, thou hast searched me, and known me. Thou knowest my downsitting and mine uprising, thou understandest my thought afar off. Thou compassest my path and my lying down, and art acquainted with all my ways. For there is not a word in my tongue, but, lo, O LORD, thou knowest it altogether. Thou hast beset me behind and before, and laid thine hand upon me. **Psalm 139:1-5**

For the ways of man are before the eyes of the LORD, and he pondereth all his goings. **Proverbs 5:21**

"God is spirit. He is a trinity of God the Father, God the Son, and God the Holy Spirit. He is also a gracious and loving God."

And the LORD passed by before him, and proclaimed, The LORD, The LORD God, merciful and gracious, longsuffering, and abundant in goodness and truth, **Exodus 34:6**

Blessed be the God and Father of our Lord Jesus Christ, which according to his abundant mercy hath begotten us again unto a lively hope by the resurrection of Jesus Christ from the dead, **1 Peter 1:3**

Beloved, let us love one another: for love is of God; and every one that loveth is born of God, and knoweth God. **1 John 4:7**

"But the one aspect of God that is so pertinent to our discussion is, He is holy. He is undefiled. He is without sin. He is pure. And that is fascinating to think about!"

And one cried unto another, and said, Holy, holy, holy, is the LORD of hosts: the whole earth is full of his glory. **Isaiah 6:3**

Thou art of purer eyes than to behold evil, and canst not look on iniquity: wherefore lookest thou upon them that deal treacherously, and holdest thy tongue when the wicked devoureth the man that is more righteous than he? **Habakkuk 1:13**

"So now it makes sense that since He is holy and He hates sin, that all I would have to do is to be sin-free, and I will be all right on Judgment Day when I meet Him. So that leads to a question: Would you consider yourself a good person?"

"Now we can definitely agree on something. Although my wife and kids and probably co-workers would say I'm not perfect, they would absolutely attest to the fact that I'm a good man. It's easy to sleep at night when so many people think well of you."

"Have you ever heard of the Ten Commandments?"

"C'mon, man. I went to twelve years of Catholic school and even a Catholic college! Those nuns drilled those into me when I was a kid!"

"Those commandments are basically a universal standard for what good is. You find them repeated in the Bible, so we know they must be very important. Have you ever told a lie before?"

Thou shalt not bear false witness against thy neighbour. **Exodus 20:16**

"Everyone has told a lie before. You are not breaking new ground here!"

"No, I am not worried about everyone else. Have *you* told a lie before?"

"A few white ones here and there, and every now and then to one of my employees, and maybe every so often when my wife asks me if I like her outfit, but beyond that hardly any at all."

"Since you have told lies before, what would that make you?"

"That makes me human! But you are probably looking for the word *sinner*. But that does not make me as bad as most people walking planet earth."

"If someone rapes, they are a rapist; if someone murders, they are a murderer. Since you have told a lie, what would that make you?"

"If you are looking for the word *liar*, okay, I will say it: Liar. But don't you have to tell a ton of lies to be a liar?"

"It only takes one murder to be a murderer. Trust me, it only takes one lie to be a liar. Have you ever stolen something before?"

"Nothing really big. I did nab a baseball from the department store one time, but a lot of the boys had fun with it. I also pilfered a few things from a convenience store by my house, but all the boys were doing it."

"Have you ever cheated on a test in school?"

"Yes, I have done that before."

"You stole an answer off someone else's test."

"Now that is a very good point! I never looked at it that way. Score one for you."

"If you steal one thing, what would that make you?"

"Well, I would say a stealer, but you might get on me for my bad use of the English language! So let's say, thief."

"Have you ever lusted in your heart before?"

"I think you can tell I am a man, can't you? Of course, I have lusted before. It is just what men do. Can't really help it, and periodically, I kind of like it."

"Jesus said even if someone looks upon a woman with lust, that is the same as committing adultery."

> *But I say unto you, That whosoever looketh on a woman to lust after her hath committed adultery with her already in his heart.*
> **Matthew 5:28**

"Okay, I have been kind of joking around a bit, but you have got me thinking. Are you serious? God is really going to judge someone if they have had lustful thoughts?"

"Remember, He is a holy God. He is pure. Never forget that He is perfect and spotless."

"Good point."

"Have you ever taken the Lord's name in vain before?"

"I would periodically lose my cool while I was playing basketball, and some words would fly out of my mouth. Also, sometimes when I was watching Notre Dame football. But I didn't mean anything by those words. They were just sayings and nothing else."

"When someone takes God's name in vain, that is called *blasphemy.* That is a very heavy sin in God's eyes. The reason is that the name of God *is* God. They are one in the same. Just like none of us will let anyone talk about our moms because Mom is Mom. It is that simple.

"Have you ever dishonored your mom and dad?" He continued.

"Are you serious? Do you think God is worried about that?"

Honour thy father and thy mother: that thy days may be long upon the land which the LORD thy God giveth thee. **Exodus 20:12**

"God is very serious about obeying our parents. If we learn to obey our parents, we will learn to obey God. If we learn to disobey our parents, we will learn to disobey God. There is an authority structure in our world, whether we like it or not."

"I have always been a rebellious sort. I have seemed to rebel against authority a lot in my past. Seems like it has been a pattern in my life, but you are right in that it really did start with my family. I would do things my parents told me not to, break curfew, etc. Yes, I have done that."

"Have you ever been angry at anyone?"

"I am a former basketball player! They should have never made referees! Of course, I have been angry at people. That is probably part of my rebelliousness as well."

"God actually says that anger without cause is the same as committing murder. I have actually done some prison ministry work and have had the chance to be on death row. It is very interesting when you talk with those men. They would get angry first, and then knife a buddy over a dice game. They would get angry first, and then shoot and kill their wife. It was amazing how their inside thoughts would lead to outside actions."

"That does make a lot of sense now that you have explained it that way."

"You just told me that you are a liar, a thief, disobedient to your parents, a blasphemer, an adulterer by lust, and a murderer by anger. So would you be guilty or not guilty on Judgment Day?"

"Hold up there, partner. I may have broken some of those commandments, but I am not Hitler! Osama bin Laden is a tad worse than I ever was. This isn't a serial killer sitting next to you."

"Remember God's holiness. One sin is like a million to Him. Impure is impure. It doesn't take a gallon of black ink to make a beautiful wedding dress tainted and unclean. It only takes one drop. Ask a bride. She knows the answer. Also, remember that God doesn't compare you against other folks on planet earth. He won't compare your goodness to anyone else's either."

For whosoever shall keep the whole law, and yet offend in one point, he is guilty of all.   **James 2:10**

"So back to that standard again, would you be guilty or not guilty on Judgment Day?"

"Wait a minute. What about all of my good works? Don't those come into play?"

As it is written, There is none righteous, no, not one: **Romans 3:10**

"Remember, that good works can only cover up your sins but can't cleanse or remove them. It is like putting white icing on a burnt cake. It looks good on the outside but tastes terrible on the inside. The icing just covered up the real problem. Each one of us truly needs to be transformed, Josh. You and I both need forgiveness and not a mask for our sins in the presence of a holy God. When someone realizes how they compare to God's holiness, they realize how wretched they are because of their sins."

Then said I, Woe is me! for I am undone; because I am a man of unclean lips, and I dwell in the midst of a people of unclean lips: for mine eyes have seen the King, the LORD of hosts.   **Isaiah 6:5**

O wretched man that I am! who shall deliver me from the body of this death?   **Romans 7:24**

197

"Guilty or not guilty on Judgment Day?"

"You make a good case. I would be guilty."

"So would that mean heaven or hell when you die?"

"If that is the standard, then it would mean hell. But that standard would mean that everyone is going to hell unless God provided a way out. He is not a very fair God if He sends everyone to hell."

"Very good point. Does it bother you that you would be going to hell?"

"If all this is true, and I am still using 'if' here, then yes, it would bother me."

"Do you know what it would take to make sure you wouldn't go there?"

"No, I don't, but I do want you to share that with me."

"You have a decision to make. You have to decide if you want to repent of your sins. Repentance is basically a change of mind that will lead to a change of actions. So ask yourself, do you want to do that? Do you want a different life?"

> *But shewed first unto them of Damascus, and at Jerusalem, and throughout all the coasts of Judaea, and then to the Gentiles, that they should repent and turn to God, and do works meet for repentance.* **Acts 26:20**

"Once you can answer yes to that, then you just need to believe in what Jesus did on the cross for you. He is the perfect sacrifice for your sins, and He rose from the dead to back up everything He said."

> *Testifying both to the Jews, and also to the Greeks, repentance toward God, and faith toward our Lord Jesus Christ.* **Acts 20:21**

> *And Philip said, If thou believest with all thine heart, thou mayest. And he answered and said, I believe that Jesus Christ is the Son of God.* **Acts 8:37**

> *Moreover, brethren, I declare unto you the gospel which I preached unto you, which also ye have received, and wherein ye stand; By*

which also ye are saved, if ye keep in memory what I preached unto you, unless ye have believed in vain. For I delivered unto you first of all that which I also received, how that Christ died for our sins according to the scriptures; And that he was buried, and that he rose again the third day according to the scriptures: And that he was seen of Cephas, then of the twelve: After that, he was seen of above five hundred brethren at once; of whom the greater part remain unto this present, but some are fallen asleep. **1 Corinthians 15:1-6**

"Jesus, being God, could not leave open to question whether He did or did not rise from the dead. That is why He had eyewitnesses there to make sure people would know the truth."

And without controversy great is the mystery of godliness: God was manifest in the flesh, justified in the Spirit, seen of angels, preached unto the Gentiles, believed on in the world, received up into glory. **1 Timothy 3:16**

"The resurrection is something to really think about. If that was a real event in history, you now have the right answer. If Jesus rose from the dead, so will you. If it did not happen, then you have to keep searching to find the right answer."

Now if Christ be preached that he rose from the dead, how say some among you that there is no resurrection of the dead? But if there be no resurrection of the dead, then is Christ not risen: And if Christ be not risen, then is our preaching vain, and your faith is also vain. Yea, and we are found false witnesses of God; because we have testified of God that he raised up Christ: whom he raised not up, if so be that the dead rise not. For if the dead rise not, then is not Christ raised: And if Christ be not raised, your faith is vain; ye are yet in your sins. **1 Corinthians 15:12-17**

"I heard some good evidence for the resurrection today. That is not my hang-up."

"When you believe in what Jesus did on the cross for your sins, your sins are literally washed away. Gone. History. There will be no sin for God to judge when you stand before Him. It's the best deal in the world! You literally get a new heart from the Lord."

And I will give them one heart, and I will put a new spirit within you; and I will take the stony heart out of their flesh, and will give them an heart of flesh: **Ezekiel 11:19**

"When Jesus said, 'It is finished,' He meant it! There is nothing else you have to do, Josh. Repent and believe, and you will be saved."

When Jesus therefore had received the vinegar, he said, It is finished: and he bowed his head, and gave up the ghost. **John 19:30**

"When you do that, you are declared guilt-free of all of the sins that you have committed. It is like being found guilty in a courtroom before a judge. The evidence was clear you were guilty of the crime, but the judge wiped away the punishment for the crime. In an eternal sense, you don't get what you deserve—hell. You get what you don't deserve—heaven. And you get to spend it with God for all of eternity."

And this is life eternal, that they might know thee the only true God, and Jesus Christ, whom thou hast sent. **John 17:3**

"Do you really think it is that simple?" I responded.

Josh is thirty minutes away from eternity. Which choice will he make?

"I really, really do."

Verily I say unto you, Whosoever shall not receive the kingdom of God as a little child, he shall not enter therein. **Mark 10:15**

As the sun starts setting, I am doing a lot of thinking.

"I want to thank you for what you just shared. So, are you saying that the same Jesus Who is painting this gorgeous color display and making this literal wonderland of paradise shine all around us, is the One I must commit my life to?"

"God demands a perfect blood sacrifice for your sins. You can hand Him nothing else. Yes, Jesus is that sacrifice that you are looking for."

"I guess I still don't understand. Why does it have to be a sacrifice?"

"God hates sin so much that He wants it put to death."

"Why does it need to be blood? Can't we offer our works or good intentions?"

"Did you know, Josh, that blood is a cleanser? It brings life-giving nourishment to your body and carries away the impurities that would cause your death. Same with the blood of Jesus. His blood can bring you His life and carry away your sin that would cause your eternal death. Nothing else can remove sin."

"I never thought about it like that before. That certainly explains things from a different angle. Last question though, why does this sacrifice need to be perfect?"

"Because a sinful person can't pay for their own sins. Only God is sinless, so He became a man to be that perfect sacrifice to be offered back to Him by faith. Nothing else will suffice. And think about this: if good works could save us, then why did Jesus have to die?"

"Now that gives me something to mull over. I really want to thank you for sitting next to me and sharing all of that with me. You have given me a lot of information to process. Thank you. I will contemplate all of this over the days and years to come."

"One other question before I go. Can you guarantee me that you are going to wake up tomorrow morning?"

"Sure I am. Well, it is not a guarantee, but I am pretty sure."

"Remember, that the Scriptures tell us that today is the day of salvation. Would you like to repent of your sins and believe upon the Lord Jesus Christ for the forgiveness of your sins?"

"I still need to think about it some. I am still at the gathering information stage, and I have garnered a lot of it today. I am still wrestling with whether my good works can get me to heaven or not. I still have time to process it all. Thank you, though."

"Have you ever thought about, what if you are wrong? What if Jesus is the only way to heaven, and what if you reject what He has done for you?"

"Well, that would mean that I would be choosing hell over heaven for all of eternity."

"Eternity is a long time to have the wrong answer. While you are still breathing on this side of eternity, you can repent and believe. But once you take that last breath, there is no changing destinations on the other side. Heaven or hell, and you will be there forever and ever and ever. We have something here called *Hawaiian time*. It means 'running late or tardy.' You will hear people use that as an excuse for being late. But remember that none of us will have Hawaiian time when we die. We will be right on time for death. The question is, will we be ready to meet the One we will see face to face on the other side?"

"Thanks again."

"One last question before the sun goes down. What is your name?"

"My name is Josh."

"Is that short for Joshua?"

"Yes."

"Do you know what your name means?"

"Actually, I do not."

"'Joshua' is one of the highest names in all of Hebrew. It is *Yehoshu'a* in Hebrew, which means '*Yahweh* is salvation.' The Greek translation of your name is *Yeshu'a*, which means 'the Lord is my salvation.' *Yeshu'a* actually translates into the word 'Jesus.' Your name, Josh, is 'Jesus,' the One Who died for your sins!"

"Are you serious? You're not kidding me, are you? Wow! That's humbling. I never, ever knew that. Thanks for telling me that."

Josh is fifteen minutes away from meeting the real Jesus.

"You are welcome. Take care. I will be praying for you."

"Before you go, what is your name if I may ask?"

"It is Christopher, but I go by Chris."

"Do you know what your name means?"

"Yes, I do. It means 'Christ-bearer' or 'light-bearer of Christ.' That is actually how I got saved, Josh. Someone back in the day told me what my name meant. I had no clue. I was really taken aback by that. So I started to do some research about who Jesus is, and once I saw all the evidence, I knew it was time to repent of my sins. I needed to believe in Him for the forgiveness of my sins. Don't miss this moment, Josh. God is trying to reach out to you in the same way. Be careful of waiting too long to make that decision and don't let anything keep you from coming to Him. You have no clue when you will be stepping into eternity."

As I watch Chris stride away, I am sitting here stunned. There is so much spinning in my head from this whole day. I need to relax and just enjoy the final moments of this sunset, and then I can process all of this after our first round of golf tomorrow.

 Josh will be meeting the real Yeshu'a in less than ten minutes, and at this moment, he is not ready for that encounter.

1.

What a sunset! *Absolutely* remarkable! This really is a spectacular place. This is exactly what I needed. I needed to rejuvenate my soul, and this trip to Paradise is going to do just that! Golf and sunsets for a week! This is just what I needed to get back on track. This week has gotten off to an amazing start. This will be the vacation of a lifetime!

> *The sun also ariseth, and the sun goeth down, and hasteth to his place where he arose.*   **Ecclesiastes 1:5**

Time for me to meander back to the hotel. I do want to take my time and relish in what I just saw. But I still have so much going through my mind. I have seen and heard so much today. My dream from last night. Did I evolve from animals or did God create me, and did He create this enormously stunning universe? Was that really an angel that protected me this morning? Is the Bible true? Do I need forgiveness for my sins or are my good works good enough to get me to heaven? Did Jesus really resurrect from the dead? How much time do I have left to make this decision? What if I am wrong?

Five minutes until Josh enters the afterlife. Eternal Paradise or the eternal Lake of Fire. Which will it be?

This is getting frustrating. I came out here for some rest and relaxation. Just to spend some time with my buddies and hit some golf balls. But now, all I have swirling around in my head

205

are thoughts about eternity. This was not in my plans for my 50th birthday. Not at all. I have more time to wrestle with this, don't I? I am not going to die anytime soon, so I can think about this tomorrow after we play golf. Two weeks ago when that co-worker died of a heart attack, it sure did make me think. He was here one moment and then gone just like that. Literally, one heartbeat away from eternity. Like they say about the vice president, he is one heartbeat away from being president, and that man was one heartbeat away from leaving this life. That funeral was tough. A wife and kids left behind. So sad. But I was amazed at how quickly I put that behind me. How was I able to do that? How can I not be thinking about a man who I worked with for all those years? Shouldn't his life and death be more in the forefront of my mind?

 Four minutes until Josh crosses over to the other side.

Will the same thing happen to me? I die, everyone comes to the funeral, and then just as quickly they forget about me like I never existed? Is that really what this life is all about?

Suddenly, I felt a hand pulling my arm. "Hey! What are you doing? Why did you put your hands on me?"

"I saw you walking toward the street. You looked to be in pretty deep thought. You didn't see that car speeding so quickly down the street. I didn't want you to step off the curb and get hit. That car would have won the battle, and it would not have been good for you," the man said.

"Thank you. That was very kind of you. Sorry for yelling at you."

Now, I remember as a kid leaving that event at the sports arena. I was one of those kids with too much energy. My dad and three boys getting ready to cross the street, but we were not at an intersection. As I started stepping out, there was suddenly a forearm in my chest. It wasn't my dad's forearm because I could look and see him. As I turned my head, there was this big man standing next to me. His forearm stopped me from crossing the street. As my head turned, I could see this sports car just zooming down the street. I was about to walk out in front of that car. That man was not going to let that happen. It would not have been a good scene if I had done that. That man cared enough to make sure this boy did not go darting across that street. And here we are years and years later, and the same thing just happened again!

"Thank you again, sir!"

This is going to drive me crazy. I am contemplating this eternal stuff way too much. Look around. We just had this great sunset, tons of people are walking the streets. Lights are on in the shops, restaurants, and clubs. This is a beautiful evening here in Waikiki. What I need to do is enjoy myself. This is my 50th birthday!! I need to get back to the hotel and find the guys and celebrate! Life is so, so good!

 The two-minute warning has sounded. Is Josh listening?

As I am heading back, I stop for a second. Look at all these people: tall, short, skinny, not so skinny, white, black, Asian, Hispanic, Americans, foreigners, rich, poor, homeless, young, middle age, and old. If all of the information I heard today is true, then all of these people are heading to either heaven or hell. They are walking towards an eternal destination, and they probably don't even know it. They are caught up here in Paradise, and the clock of life is winding down. We worry about being married or single, do we have a job, can we pay the bills, why does my sports team keep losing, will I leave any money for the kids, do I have the right car or live in the right neighborhood, etc. But will any of that matter when I die? Is it all forgotten at death, or is it all remembered? If there is a black box like a plane has, that records everything that happened in my life, then I have a lot that I am accountable for before Almighty God.

Neither is there any creature that is not manifest in his sight: but all things are naked and opened unto the eyes of him with whom we have to do.   **Hebrews 4:13**

But I know I am a good person. Good is what counts here, and good is what must count when we die. It just makes sense. And if there is one thing that I have been in this lifetime, it is logical, and I don't plan on losing that logic at this point in my life. I can't be wrong about this, can I?

There is a way which seemeth right unto a man, but the end thereof are the ways of death.   **Proverbs 14:12**

Oh, no. The street preachers have moved! Now I have to pass them as I get to the hotel. I don't want to cross the street to avoid them because that hasn't gone so well. Hopefully, they will be busy with other folks as I walk by in a few seconds. Let me wait a minute. I can see their signs from here. They have some different ones. "TRUST JESUS." Okay, I have heard that today. "GOD HATES SIN." Yes, He is a holy God. That was abundantly clear from what Chris told me. But He is forgiving, so He will forgive my little sins, won't He?

The foolish shall not stand in thy sight: thou hatest all workers of iniquity.   **Psalm 5:5**

Another one says, "GOD IS ANGRY WITH THE WICKED EVERY DAY." That can't be the God of the Bible, can it? I am not that wicked. Chris did tell me that one sin makes me impure and unclean on the inside. But still, how can God see me as wicked? I am a good guy. Period.

...God is angry with the wicked every day.   **Psalms 7:11**

One banner just says, "REPENT."

From that time Jesus began to preach, and to say, Repent: for the kingdom of heaven is at hand.   **Matthew 4:17**

I tell you, Nay: but, except ye repent, ye shall all likewise perish.
Luke 13:3

Or despisest thou the riches of his goodness and forbearance and longsuffering; not knowing that the goodness of God leadeth thee to repentance?
Romans 2:4

These guys are either crazy or they know what they are talking about. I feel like my brain is about to explode. It is like information overload, but at the same time very simple. Either He is holy and I need forgiveness and the cross of Jesus Christ provides that, or no matter what is out there, my good works will be my ticket on the other side.

Time to walk past them.

"Hey, Josh. I just wanted to let you know that I was praying for you after you left," Jose said.

"Why did you do that?"

"Because I care about your soul and I care where you will spend eternity."

I could tell he meant that. "Thanks, Jose, and thanks for the prayers."

"What have you decided to do with what we talked about today, Josh?"

"Still processing it. Still gathering information. I will make a decision sometime soon."

 60 seconds.

"Remember, Josh, that no decision is a decision. If you don't say 'yes' to what Jesus has done, you have then said 'no.' There is no middle ground here. All of these people you see tonight are either lost or saved. Those are the only two categories on planet earth. It is that simple. You are in the lost category, Josh. It is time to get into the saved category."

"I hear you, Jose. You make good points."

"Michael made the right decision today, Josh. It is a choice each one of us makes. Can you guarantee me that you are going to wake up tomorrow morning?"

I seem to be getting that question a lot. "No. I have time to make this decision. No one dies on their 50th birthday!"

And the serpent said unto the woman, Ye shall not surely die:
Genesis 3:4

"Please, Josh, I am begging you. I can see it in your eyes. You know this is true, and you know Jesus is the right answer. Today is the day of salvation. You have no clue if you are going to cross that street tonight and still be alive. A car can hit you at any moment. A heart attack can consume you at a moment's notice. And whenever that moment happens, you will be in the presence of God."

We are confident, I say, and willing rather to be absent from the body, and to be present with the Lord. **2 Corinthians 5:8**

"Please, Josh. Heed what I am saying to you."

"Thanks again." And I was gone. I know that man cares about me, and I appreciate it. But I don't plan on ruining this birthday by getting all spiritual. Now is not the time. I have a nice house, a good family, and a good retirement plan that will kick in soon. I am okay.

And he spake a parable unto them, saying, The ground of a certain rich man brought forth plentifully: And he thought within himself, saying, What shall I do, because I have no room where to bestow my fruits? And he said, This will I do: I will pull down my barns, and build greater; and there will I bestow all my fruits and my goods. And I will say to my soul, Soul, thou hast much goods laid up for many years; take thine ease, eat, drink, and be merry. But God said unto him, Thou fool, this night thy soul shall be required of thee: then whose shall those things be, which thou hast provided? So is he that layeth up treasure for himself, and is not rich toward God. **Luke 12:16-21**

As I walk away, I am still pondering all that has happened today. So much to think about. Is it Jesus or is it my works? My choice. What if these people I met today are right? What have I accomplished in 50 years that would have any meaning before God? I was nice to my wife and kids, and made some money, and volunteered a little bit, and didn't tick off too many people? But what would Jesus have to say about all that? Why do I get the feeling He wouldn't be too impressed with those meager accomplishments? I have to make a decision. Lost or saved. One or the other. Arghhh! This is so conflicting, but I know deep down that I am a good guy. Everyone tells me that. How could God reject me? I don't think He can. I am going to rest upon my good works. I know that is the right answer. I can't be wrong. They will get me where I want to go in this life and in the life to come. Settled. Finally. It is almost like a weight has been lifted off my shoulders. I am excited. I am so glad that people are trusting Jesus for their salvation. I also know tons of us who are trusting in our works as well. It will all work out in the end. We will all wind up in the same place.

 45 seconds until physical death.

As I head to the hotel, it is just around the corner. So much to think about. What a fun twenty-four hours it has been here in Hawaii so far! This is really turning into a dream trip. I really never thought I would do so much thinking about spiritual matters on my 50th birthday, but I have somewhat enjoyed it. Now a good night's sleep and I will be ready to hit the links. Going to get a chance to work on my golf game a bit. Thank goodness I have time for that and many other things. It needs the work, so I might as well work on it in Paradise!

In whose hand is the soul of every living thing, and the breath of all mankind.   **Job 12:10**

30 seconds until departure.

As I turn the corner, someone catches my eye in front of the hotel. No, it couldn't be. That is my wife! What is she doing here? Those are my kids!! What is going on? Michael! I knew he was up to no good. He flew all of them out here to surprise me?! That is just like that guy. I have always liked him. What a guy! So that is why I haven't heard from them all day. This is the best surprise anyone could ever have! They are even loaded with presents. This is crazy. Life is so good! It makes me want to cry. I love them all so very much!

Wait a minute. Who is that guy walking toward them? He is pulling a gun!

"No! No!! No!!! Not my wife and kids!"

5, "Don't shoot!!"

4, "Don't shoot!!!"

3, Bang. Bang. Bang.

2, 1, 0, *Eternity* . . . .

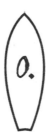

0, 1, 2, 3, 4, 5 . . . Oh, this is not good. I am still alive! Oh, wait! This is uncomfortable. No, more than that, this is unbearable! Wait, where am I? It's dark. This is not okay. The heat is oppressive and intolerable. Oh this is bad, really bad. What did I do? What did I not do? It was Jesus all along. He is the Creator, and I didn't repent and believe. Oh please, don't I get a second chance? Can I repent of my sins and believe now? Oh no! I am lost forever and ever and ever. That *was* an angel that protected me, so I could hear the truth. Jose was correct. So was Chris. Michael made the right decision, and I did not. Oh God, get me out of here! But it isn't going to happen. I now know it won't. Oh please, God, if you can hear me, please, please, please don't let my wife and kids come here. Jesus, don't let Alex and Daniel come here either. Someone needs to talk with my family about Jesus *now*! Let them listen to Michael and what he says.

Oh, no!!! This is like *déjà vu*. I'll be like one of those people in my dream standing in line before His throne. The books will be opened, and I will be judged according to my deeds! My sins have not been washed away! I will be found guilty for my sins! And that means this torment is never going to end, is it? I have just made the biggest mistake I have ever made in my life, and now I will have all of eternity to pay for it. The Lake of Fire will be next for me. I cannot believe I rejected what Jesus did for me, and it was right before my eyes. Works? I really thought works was the answer? What an absolute fool that I am. This is just the beginning of where I absolutely don't want to be . . . forever! *No!! NO!!! NOOOOOOO!!!!!*

You see, Josh is still alive. He is now alive on the other side. Death is not the end. The problem, though, is that he is alive in hell. He is screaming. He is in agony. He played a game with God and lost. He knew there were eternal consequences when he walked off planet earth. He did not heed the call of those who warned him. That was his choice. And he made a horrible decision that will last forever and ever and ever. It was Paradise lost for Josh. What will it be for you? Eternity is not a game. Eternity and hell are not a joke. People are heading there today as you read this book. You will be heading there as well if you don't commit your life to Jesus Christ. It is time to trust Jesus as your Savior.

Will you be like Josh and reject what Jesus has done for you? Put the decision off? He had ample opportunity to search this out and get saved, but he chose not to. He came face to face with the facts many times but decided not to believe the evidence. Was it coincidence that he was given so much information his last day of life? So many warnings? That everywhere he turned he was being urged to make the one decision his eternity would hang on?

What will they say at Josh's funeral? He was a "good man"? That is good, but they cannot say he was saved. By the way, what will they say at your funeral?

Or will you be like Michael and repent and believe upon the Lord Jesus Christ for the forgiveness of your sins?

Eternity is rushing toward each one of us. Will we face that reality or ignore it? The problem is that Josh chose the wrong Paradise.

And there were also two other, malefactors, led with him to be put to death. And when they were come to the place, which is called Calvary, there they crucified him, and the malefactors, one on the right hand, and the other on the left. Then said Jesus, Father, forgive them; for they know not what they do. And they parted his raiment, and cast lots. And the people stood beholding.

And the rulers also with them derided him, saying, He saved others; let him save himself, if he be Christ, the chosen of God. And the soldiers also mocked him, coming to him, and offering him vinegar, And saying, If thou be the king of the Jews, save thyself. And a superscription also was written over him in letters of Greek, and Latin, and Hebrew, THIS IS THE KING OF THE JEWS. And one of the malefactors which were hanged railed on him, saying, If thou be Christ, save thyself and us. But the other answering rebuked him, saying, Dost not thou fear God, seeing thou art in the same condemnation? And we indeed justly; for we receive the due reward of our deeds: but this man hath done nothing amiss. And he said unto Jesus, Lord, remember me when thou comest into thy kingdom. And Jesus said unto him, Verily I say unto thee, To day shalt thou be with me in paradise. **Luke 23:32-43**

Paradise is not here on this planet, even if you are in the most beautiful place on earth. In this world, each one of us is just passing through. We are headed to the other side. Jesus promises the real Paradise to those who come to Him. Look around you. Look at this grand universe that you sit in. Marvel at it just like Josh did. But remember, as great as this place is, Paradise on the other side is literally going to be mind-blowing!

And the twelve gates were twelve pearls; every several gate was of one pearl: and the street of the city was pure gold, as it were transparent glass. And I saw no temple therein: for the Lord God Almighty and the Lamb are the temple of it. And the city had no need of the sun, neither of the moon, to shine in it: for the glory of God did lighten it, and the Lamb is the light thereof. And the nations of them which are saved shall walk in the light of it: and the kings of the earth do bring their glory and honour into it. And the gates of it shall not be shut at all by day: for there shall be no night there. And they shall bring the glory and honour of the nations into it. And there shall in no wise enter into it any thing that defileth, neither whatsoever worketh abomination, or maketh a lie: but they which are written in the Lamb's book of life. **Revelation 21:21-27**

And I heard a great voice out of heaven saying, Behold, the tabernacle of God is with men, and he will dwell with them, and they shall be his people, and God himself shall be with them, and be their God. And God shall wipe away all tears from their eyes; and there shall be no more death, neither sorrow, nor crying, neither shall there be any more pain: for the former things are passed away. And he that sat upon the throne said, Behold, I make all things new. And he said unto me, Write: for these words are true and faithful. And he said unto me, It is done. I am Alpha and Omega, the beginning and the end. I will give unto him that is athirst of the fountain of the water of life freely. He that overcometh shall inherit all things; and I will be his God, and he shall be my son.   **Revelation 21:3-7**

But you are still here under the sun. You can do something about your destiny. The choice is yours. Repent and believe, and you will one day be in Paradise. Or choose to go off into eternity without Jesus Christ, and it is hell forever and ever and ever.

Please let us know what decision you have made at: mydecision@markcahill.org.

Now, if you are born again and saved, what do you plan to do with your life? Do you plan on warning the Joshes of the world about the Judgment to come? Will you be like Michael and witness to them? Will you be faithful like those street preachers, the people handing out tracts, and Chris who took time to witness to Josh? God is looking for faithful people, and He uses faithful people all the time for His eternal purposes!

His lord said unto him, Well done, thou good and faithful servant: thou hast been faithful over a few things, I will make thee ruler over many things: enter thou into the joy of thy lord.   **Matthew 25:21**

And he saith unto them, Why are ye fearful, O ye of little faith? Then he arose, and rebuked the winds and the sea; and there was a great calm.   **Matthew 8:26**

(For we walk by faith, not by sight:)   **2 Corinthians 5:7**

Who is going to witness to Josh's wife and kids? It will have to be someone who is faithful. I will guarantee you that Michael will. It also won't be Michael's last conversation with Alex and Daniel either. Will Michael share the gospel at Josh's funeral? You know he will. Why? You can tell in a short time that he is a faithful man.

You can see him being faithful all the days of his life. His life is going to end well. How will you finish the race of life?

> *I have fought a good fight, I have finished my course, I have kept the faith: Henceforth there is laid up for me a crown of righteousness, which the Lord, the righteous judge, shall give me at that day: and not to me only, but unto all them also that love his appearing.* **2 Timothy 4:7,8**

Remember, that when it comes to God, you will either finish strong or you will finish wrong. It is really that simple.

> *Then saith he unto his disciples, The harvest truly is plenteous, but the labourers are few; Pray ye therefore the Lord of the harvest, that he will send forth labourers into his harvest.* **Matthew 9:37,38**

> *Whosoever therefore shall confess me before men, him will I confess also before my Father which is in heaven. But whosoever shall deny me before men, him will I also deny before my Father which is in heaven. Think not that I am come to send peace on earth: I came not to send peace, but a sword. For I am come to set a man at variance against his father, and the daughter against her mother, and the daughter in law against her mother in law. And a man's foes shall be they of his own household. He that loveth father or mother more than me is not worthy of me: and he that loveth son or daughter more than me is not worthy of me. And he that taketh not his cross, and followeth after me, is not worthy of me. He that findeth his life shall lose it: and he that loseth his life for my sake shall find it.* **Matthew 10:32-39**

Paradise's parents were wrong. Family, friends, and relationships are not the high point of this life. It is being born from above. The new life in Jesus Christ is what you are here to find and live. Everything else is just window dressing.

> *And as they did eat, he said, Verily I say unto you, that one of you shall betray me. And they were exceeding sorrowful, and began every one of them to say unto him, Lord, is it I? And he answered and said, He that dippeth his hand with me in the dish, the same shall betray me. The Son of man goeth as it is written of him: but*

woe unto that man by whom the Son of man is betrayed! it had been good for that man if he had not been born. Then Judas, which betrayed him, answered and said, Master, is it I? He said unto him, Thou hast said. **Matthew 26:21-25**

What would you betray Jesus for? Tickets to see your college football team, a dollar bill, Paradise, thirty pieces of silver? Why when I speak around the country do I see so many cars in church parking lots with the flags, bumper stickers, etc. for their college sports teams? Are those same people being soul winners for the Lord during the week? The price of salvation was costly. How high is *that* banner being held? Or will we stand more for our sports team than we do for our God? Do we say, "Go Dawgs," "Geaux Tigers," "War Eagle," "Roll Tide," "Go Jackets," etc. more than we say the name of Jesus?

Whosoever therefore shall be ashamed of me and of my words in this adulterous and sinful generation; of him also shall the Son of man be ashamed, when he cometh in the glory of his Father with the holy angels. **Mark 8:38**

For though I preach the gospel, I have nothing to glory of: for necessity is laid upon me; yea, woe is unto me, if I preach not the gospel! **1 Corinthians 9:16**

This is no time to be lukewarm. It is time to be fired-up for what Jesus has done for you. Open up your mouth and go tell someone! He gave you His all. Will you do the same?

So then because thou art lukewarm, and neither cold nor hot, I will spue thee out of my mouth. **Revelation 3:16**

It is time to be a watchman for the Lord. Pick up the trumpet and blow it as loud and clear as you can in the days to come. Time is short. People need to be ready. Tomorrow just might be too late.

But if the watchman see the sword come, and blow not the trumpet, and the people be not warned; if the sword come, and take any person from among them, he is taken away in his iniquity; but his blood will I require at the watchman's hand. **Ezekiel 33:6**

Behold, I shew you a mystery; We shall not all sleep, but we shall all be changed, In a moment, in the twinkling of an eye, at the last trump: for the trumpet shall sound, and the dead shall be raised incorruptible, and we shall be changed. For this corruptible must put on incorruption, and this mortal must put on immortality. So when this corruptible shall have put on incorruption, and this mortal shall have put on immortality, then shall be brought to pass the saying that is written, Death is swallowed up in victory. O death, where is thy sting? O grave, where is thy victory? The sting of death is sin; and the strength of sin is the law. But thanks be to God, which giveth us the victory through our Lord Jesus Christ. Therefore, my beloved brethren, be ye stedfast, unmoveable, always abounding in the work of the Lord, forasmuch as ye know that your labour is not in vain in the Lord.   **1 Corinthians 15:51-58**

Paradise is real. You want EVERYONE to be there when they die.

And the lord said unto the servant, Go out into the highways and hedges, and compel them to come in, that my house may be filled.   **Luke 14:23**

How that he was caught up into paradise, and heard unspeakable words, which it is not lawful for a man to utter. **2 Corinthians 12:4**

He that hath an ear, let him hear what the Spirit saith unto the churches; To him that overcometh will I give to eat of the tree of life, which is in the midst of the paradise of God. **Revelation 2:7**

You want to make sure you have picked the right Paradise, and you are bringing people to that right Paradise. And trust me, it is not here.

This poem is pretty powerful. Be careful before you read it.

My Friend

My friend, I stand in judgment now
And feel that you're to blame somehow
While on this earth I walked with you day by day
And never did you point the way

You knew the Lord in truth and glory
But never did you tell the story
My knowledge then was very dim
You could have led me safe to him

Though we lived together here on earth
You never told me of your second birth
And now I stand this day condemned
Because you failed to mention him

You taught me many things, that's true
I called you friend and trusted you
But now I learned, now it's too late
You could have kept me from this fate

We walked by day and talked by night
And yet you showed me not the light
You let me live, love and die
And all the while you knew I'd never live on high

Yes, I called you friend in life
And trusted you in joy and strife
Yet in coming to this end
I see you really weren't my friend [68]

Will you be like Remo and Kaiya and not share your faith with the Joshes of the world? Will you only go so far, but not all the way? I know for a fact that if Remo and Kaiya had known that Josh would be dead in 24 hours, they would have boldly proclaimed Jesus to him. But that is the part of the equation we will never know. You have friends that need to hear from you today. What are you going to do about it? It is time to be a bold soul winner. There are no excuses that will work on Judgment Day for not being one.

> *Watch therefore, for ye know neither the day nor the hour wherein the Son of man cometh.*   **Matthew 25:13**

Daniel didn't want what Jesus had done for them brought up in conversation again so that they could keep their friendship going. But wait a minute. What is friendship? We just hang out for 30 or 50 years and then we go to different places for all of eternity? I want eternal friendships. How about you? Thankfully, Daniel has another day to think hard about Josh checking out of life so abruptly. It could have just as easily been him. Now it is Daniel who has all the evidence before him. He can check his phone if the gravity of life and death grab his attention. What decision will he make? What decision will *you* make?

It is not enough to be like Alex and merely separate from what you know to be untruth. You must come the rest of the way to Jesus the Truth, recognize sin for being a serious offense against Almighty God, and throw the entire weight of your faith upon His sacrifice for sins: your sins, my sins and the sins of the entire world.

> *For God so loved the world, that he gave his only begotten Son, that whosoever believeth in him should not perish, but have everlasting life.*   **John 3:16**

Are you getting ready for the *real* Paradise? The choice is *yours*. Are you getting others ready for *that* Paradise? The choice is *yours*. The clock is ticking. Do you hear it? Time is running out. You will meet Jesus very soon. Josh didn't get a "do-over" for his life, and neither will you. What will it be?

5, 4, 3, 2, 1, 0, Eternity . . . .

ENDNOTES

1 U.S. Abortion Statistics, <*http://www.abort73.com/abortion_facts/us_abortion_statistics/*>

2 Do You Know The Hard Facts About Abortion In America?,<*http://www.cirtl.org/abfacts.htm*>

3 Fearfully and Wonderfully Made, The First Nine Months,<*http://www.cirtl.org/unborn.htm*>

4 160 Million and Counting, <*http://www.nytimes.com/2011/06/27/opinion/27douthat.html*>

5 Jason and Ron Carlson, Is the Bible the Inspired Word of God?, <*http://www.christianministriesintl.org/articles/Bible-the-Inspired-Word-of-God.php*>

6 Bryant Wood, In What Ways Have the Discoveries of Archaeology Verified the Reliability of the Bible?, <*http://christiananswers.net/q-abr/abr-a008.html*>

7 <*http://www.reasons.org/articles/articles/fulfilled-prophecy-evidence-for-the-reliability-of-the-bible*>

8 Mary Fairchild, 44 Prophecies Jesus Christ Fulfilled, <*http://christianity.about.com/od/biblefactsandlists/a/Prophecies-Jesus.htm*>

9 National Memorial Cemetery of the Pacific, US Department of Veterans Affairs, <*http://www.cem.va.gov/CEMs/nchp/nmcp.asp#gi*>

10 Cemetery History & Map of Punchbowl, Acres of Honor, <*http://acresofhonor.com/history.html*>

11 Alfred Henry Ackley, < *http://www.greatchristianhymns.com/he-lives.html*>

12 Mark Allwood, Watch Night services celebrate the Emancipation Proclamation in 1863, <*http://www.islandpacket.com/2008/12/27/708413/watch-night-services-celebrate.html* >

13 George Bennard, <*http://www.hymnlyrics.org/newlyrics_t/the_old_rugged_cross.php*>

14 John Newton, <*http://www.hymnlyrics.org/mostpopularhymns/amazinggrace.php*>

15 Kathie Fry, Guide to the Waikiki HistoricTrail,<*http://www.hawaiiforvisitors.com/oahu/attractions/waikiki-historic-trail.htm*>

16 Kathie Fry, Duke Kahanamoku Statue, <*http://www.hawaiiforvisitors.com/oahu/attractions/waikiki-historic-trail-05.htm*>

17 Kathie Fry, Apuakehau Stream and Waikiki Beachboys, <*http://www.hawaiiforvisitors.com/oahu/attractions/waikiki-historic-trail-11.htm*>

18 Kathie Fry, Afong Villa and Hawaii Army Museum, <*http://www.hawaiiforvisitors.com/oahu/attractions/waikiki-historic-trail-14.htm*>

19 The Merrie Monarch King David Kalakaua,<*http://www.aloha-hawaii.com/hawaii/king-kalakaua/*>

20 The Kahala Hotel & Resort, Hoku's, <*http://www.kahalaresort.com/dining/hoku.cfm*>

21 Dr. Scott Huse, *The Collapse of Evolution*, 2d ed. (Grand Rapids, MI: Baker Book House, 1993), 71–72.

22 THE CREATOR'S HANDIWORK: The Earth, Evolution Encyclopedia, Vol 2, Ch 8, <*http://evolutionfacts.com/Ev-V1/1evlch08.htm*>

23 Galileo, <*http://www.proofthatgodexists.org/favourite-quotes.php*>

24 Author Unknown, Ibid.

25 Douglas Wilson, Ibid.

26 Michel De Montaigne, Ibid.

27 George Carlin, <*http://www.1-funny-quotes.com/funny-god-quotes.html*>

28 Woody Allen, Ibid.

29 Friedrich Nietzsche, Ibid

30 P.J.O'Rourke, <*http://www.workinghumor.com/quotes/god.shtml*>

31 Joseph Heller, Ibid.

32 George Burns, Ibid.

33 Josh McDowell, Evidence for the Resurrection, <*http://www.leaderu.com/everystudent/easter/articles/josh2.html*>

34 Simon Greenleaf, *An Examination of the Testimony of the Four Evangelists by the Rules of Evidence Administered in the Courts of Justice*, p.29.

35 Dr. Terry Watkins, Th.D. <*http://www.av1611.org/resur.html*>

36 Adapted from "Questions for Evolutionists" <*http://www.drdino.com/articles.php?spec=76*>

37 Mary Leakey, Associated Press, December 10, 1996, <*http://www.atenizo.org/evolution-quotes.htm*>

38 Stephen Jay Gould, "Evolution's Erratic Pace", Natural History Vol. 5, May 1977, Ibid.

39 Dr. Stephen J. Gould, Evolution Now, p. 140, Ibid.

40 David M. Raup, "Evolution and the Fossil Record", Science, Vol. 213, July 17, 1981, p. 289, Ibid.

41 Dr. Colin Paterson, Ibid.

42 Stephen Hawking, October 19, 1997, Ibid.

43 US News and World Report, December 4, 1995, Ibid.

44 Grant R. Jeffery, *The Signature of God*, Ibid.

45 Sir Fredrick Hoyle, Cambridge University. Ibid.

46 Sir Arthur Keith, *Evolution and Ethics,* Ibid.

47 Sir Arthur Keith, Ibid.

48 Professor Louis Bounoure, Ibid.

49 Malcolm Muggeridge, Ibid.

50 Richard Dawkins, <*http://www.beliefnet.com/News/Science-Religion/2005/11/The-Problem-With-God-Interview-With-Richard-Dawkins.aspx?p=2*>

51 CarlSagan, <*http://en.thinkexist.com/search/searchquotation.asp?search=evolution&page=1,*>

52 Charles Darwin,<*http://www.overcomeproblems.com/darwin.htm*>

53 Charles Darwin, *Origin of Species*, Ch. 6, p144, Ibid.

54 The Revolution Against Evolution, <*http://www.rae.org/pdf/revev5.pdf*>

55 Ibid.

56 SCIENTIFIC FACTS AGAINST EVOLUTION, <*http://evolutionfacts.com/nature3.htm*>

57 Ibid.

58 Ibid.

59 Dr. Robert Kofahl, Quoted by Dr. Jobe Martin, *The Evolution of a Creationist,* p.106.

60 Dragonfly Vision Could Aid Robot Flight, Science Alert, Jan. 28, 2009

61 Seeing the Non-Existent, by David Cloud, email

62 <*http://evolutionfacts.com/Ev-V3/3evlch36.htm*>

63 <*http://listverse.com/2008/06/10/top-15-amazing-facts-about-the-human-body/*>

64 Anonymous, <*http://www.famous-quotes.com/topic.php?tid=413*>

65 Willhelm Bölsche,<*http://creation.com/german-scientists-at-first-laughed-at-darwin*>

66 <*http://www.to-hawaii.com/hawaiian-sunsets.php*>

67 Evangelical Tract Distributors, Distributors, P. O. Box 145, Edmonton, Alberta, T5J2G9

68 <*http:www.evangelicaloutreach.org/friend.htm*>

Mark Cahill has a business degree from Auburn University, where he was an honorable mention Academic All-American in basketball. He has worked in the business world at IBM and in various management positions, and he taught high school for four years. Mark now speaks to thousands of people a year at conferences, camps, retreats, etc. He has also appeared on numerous radio and television shows.

Mark's favorite thing to do is to go out and meet people and find out what they believe and why they believe it. You can find Mark at malls, concerts, art and music festivals, airports, beaches, sporting events, bar sections of towns, college campuses, etc., doing just that.

To arrange a speaking engagement, contact the **Ambassador Agency** toll-free at 877-425-4700 or www.ambassadoragency.com

•

To order additional books or resources, or to receive a free e-newsletter **www.markcahill.org**

•

Contact Mark Cahill at:
P.O. Box 81, Stone Mountain, GA 30086
800-NETS-158 / 800-638-7158
Email: mark@markcahill.org